JOURNEY AND STRUGGLE

JOURNEY AND STRUGGLE

FINDING THE NEXT CHAPTER

BILLY BOB BROWN JR.

NEW DEGREE PRESS
COPYRIGHT © 2020 BILLY BOB BROWN JR.
All rights reserved.

JOURNEY AND STRUGGLE
Finding the Next Chapter

ISBN   978-1-64137-459-0 *Paperback*
              978-1-64137-460-6 *Kindle Ebook*
              978-1-64137-461-3 *Ebook*

CONTENTS

	HOW TO READ THIS BOOK	7
	INTRODUCTION	9

SECTION 1.	**PURPOSE**	**19**
CHAPTER 1.	BE ALIVE!	21
CHAPTER 2.	TO SEE AND TO BE SEEN	31
CHAPTER 3.	FINDING JOY IN SORROW	41
CHAPTER 4.	DREAM DESPITE THE BUMPS AND BRUISES	51
CHAPTER 5.	IDEAS, LIKE SEEDS, NEED LOVE TO GROW	61
CHAPTER 6.	I LOST EVERYTHING	71
CHAPTER 7.	WE MUST DO SOMETHING	81
CHAPTER 8.	IT IS THE PEOPLE, NOT THE POSITION	89

SECTION 2.	**PASSION**	**99**
CHAPTER 9.	FINDING PURPOSE AT CAMP	101
CHAPTER 10.	AGE IS ONLY A NUMBER	111
CHAPTER 11.	FEAR AND LOYALTY	117
CHAPTER 12.	SEE IT IN YOUR MIND AND CREATE	125
CHAPTER 13.	PASSION'S REAL STORY	131

SECTION 3.	**PROGRESS**	**139**
CHAPTER 14.	CONSIDER – THEN DREAM	141
CHAPTER 15.	INNOVATION AND THE PASSIONATE	147

SECTION 4.	**PEOPLE**	**153**
CHAPTER 16.	PRIORITY – 177 PEOPLE	155
CHAPTER 17.	FIRST TEARS, THEN A FRESH START	163
CHAPTER 18.	TEARS UPON SEEING THE NEED	175
CHAPTER 19.	TOUCH IS THE DIFFERENCE	183
	CONCLUSION	191
	ACKNOWLEDGMENTS	195
	BIBLIOGRAPHY	197

HOW TO READ THIS BOOK

Think of this book like a pallet of paint colors. Below are some navigation aids to help you find the direction that will be most helpful:

CONSIDER WHAT YOU ARE LOOKING FOR IN THIS BOOK
Having a clear idea of the outcome you are seeking is a powerful consideration that leads to amazing results. This entire book is about understanding your own journey by observing mine. Learn from my mistakes, then go and make your own. Your journey will be more satisfying and deliberate. So start right now. **Write down three questions that you want this book to help you answer for yourself.** Now, go look for those helpful aids to navigate to the answers you seek.

THE STRUCTURE IS ONLY A GUIDE
The structure of the book is only a framework and is a non-linear approach to discovery. Do not let structure hold you back. Jump around, find something interesting and camp there with your own thoughts and ideas as you interact with what you read.

SKIP LIBERALLY
Treat each of the chapters in the book as separate and distinct, each independent, like a buoy.

Do not be pressured into a need to finish this book. Sometimes, it is the one buoy that helps get you back to safe waters and allows you to continue your journey. Like juggling a cotton ball in a tornado, my thoughts as I wrestle with ideas may appear to be written like a whirlwind. In my mind, all of the non-linear ideas are perfectly aligned. Many of the chapters are connected by theme. Some are even connected by topics or ideas but most of them stand completely by themselves. Read the ones that interest you or meet your current curiosity. Let those guide you to action.

You will not hurt my feelings if you skip whatever doesn't grab your attention. Remember the outcome you are seeking and select the chapters that may offer insights to serve you as aids.

MOVE AHEAD!
Live life! Be alive! Knowledge is powerful, but it only yields results when it results in action. Make a list for yourself from the aids you found helpful and then go out and chart your own journey.

INTRODUCTION

Your purpose in life is to find your purpose and give your whole heart and soul to it.

—BUDDHA

I expect more of myself, but is that fair?

In 2015, I listened to a sermon by Charles Swindoll and was immediately moved:

The world can be viewed as one thousand people in total. Eight hundred live in the valley. And in the valley, there is not enough food for everyone, so many go to bed at night hungry. In the valley, transportation resources are scarce—barely a vehicle available to one in every ten. In the valley, living accommodations and construction are limited to one room for every twelve people.

But two hundred live on the hill, and food is plentiful. On the hill, everyone has their fill and food is thrown away every single day. On the hill, transportation is abundant, more than

1.5 vehicles per person. And construction is in no short supply, enough for five rooms per person.

As an American, I realized I am clearly on the hill and in the land of plenty.

As an entrepreneur and technologist, I realized I have the drive and access to the tools necessary to help the people in the valley.

And yet as a human being, I realized I am not putting any resources or tools into action.

I expect more of myself, and yes, it is fair because I have more than enough to give.

***

In April 2018, while on a trip arranged by David's Hope International, I met a pastor named Steve and his wife Mary.

Their story inspired me to not only expect more but find a way to *do* more.

I was most struck by their singularity of focus and purpose: **"Reduce child malnutrition for the children in the Mt. Eburru villages."**

In its simplicity, their purpose and how they put it into action is extraordinary. They had the strength of conviction to leave their home and well-paying positions in Nairobi and move to a remote village to live out their purpose.

I can still see their faces as they told the story and the resolution of their commitment. They became missionaries in their home country to a people not their own, enduring hardship and poverty in the process.

This is unity. This is focus. This is purpose.

***

Kenya sits astride the equator, a beautiful country with more than 47 million people. More than forty tribes comprise the rich tapestry of people in Kenya, but a less-than-stable democratic philosophy undergirds the nature of power and government. However, Kenya is susceptible to the same ethnocentric preferences found in other countries, and the tribal alliance in modern Kenyan society is just as complicated as it is around the world.

In this semi-remote setting lives a small group of fewer than 15,000 villagers. Many are incredibly hard-working, dedicated, and resilient to the hardships they must endure.

This is the setting in which I met Pastor Steve and Mary. They were born and raised in Kenya but grew up in different villages, different small tribal groups. So when they decided to help villagers in Mt. Eburru, they decided to dedicate their lives to a people group not their own. At times, they remind those they serve, saying, "We are not from here, but we have *chosen* to remain here with you."

In their youth, Steve and Mary strived for opportunity. They eventually made their way to college and into great-paying jobs in Nairobi. They each took positions in the country's largest medical facility, Kijabi Hospital. Mary became a leading charge nurse and Pastor Steve became a lead chaplain.

In 2003, while Pastor Steve was debriefing a team that had journeyed to the Mt. Eburru area, he learned of the exceptionally heart-warming people. He decided to travel to Eburru to meet them, and his heart was moved by seeing the malnutrition among the children.

Steve changed his schedule, left his job, and moved to Eburru. He worked there during the week and then went home to Nairobi on the weekends. In 2006, his family joined him in Eburru.

A congregation in America sponsored him with a few thousand dollars, and he used it to expand what he then called Camp Brethren, which enabled him to formally accept orphans in the school and to recruit teachers to help.

By 2009, Mary saw the fruit of their labor. Camp Brethren had grown to consistently help five or six children through their efforts and twenty other children on the periphery.

And then, in the same year, a small group of Westerners came to Kenya and was so inspired that upon their return to the United States, they formed the non-profit David's Hope International, named for one of the children they met. The organization is exclusively dedicated to raising resources to aid Pastor Steve and Mary in their focused mission work.

Pastor Steve and Mary have given their lives for this cause, and they have far exceeded their initial goals. They have since expanded the number of children they can help, but they are still laser-focused on child malnutrition.

***

As I thought back to the words of Charles Swindoll, my own passionate concern rekindled: *Why can't those on the hill share with those in the valley? There may not be enough for everyone, but we should be able to make things more level.*

Here in front of me was a pure example. It caused me to wonder how people like Steve and Mary have such a clear purpose in their lives, when I—clearly living on the hill—do not. I realized doing nothing was unacceptable.

I have to change. I have to be part of the solution to help the eight hundred. I don't even know who the eight hundred are, but I will find them and do something to help.

***

I began to scribble and write incessantly. As an entrepreneur, technologist, and American with incredible resources, how could I best position myself to help? I could do so many things to help; it actually made me feel more overwhelmed—more helpless and less clear about what I could do.

This book was created to share my own framework of how I learned to help.

Not all help is created equal, not all impact is the same, and each of us is on a different journey. But my own experience and perspectives forced me to ask, how can I use the power of innovation to help maximize the benefit to others?

This led to the development of the 4Ps of Innovation: **Purpose, Passion, & Progress through People**

In 2018, I set June 2020 as the time to decide whether to leave the traditional "for-profit" workforce for the nonprofit sector, becoming part of the solution, and that's scary.

Having something both tangible and real means I also need to be tangible and real about how to make such a decision worthwhile.

Yes, practically, this may mean downsizing and potentially moving to where the need is the greatest. But how, where, and why does that happen?

This book is a part of that journey, a collection of stories, insights, and anecdotes designed to detail my own journey to not only *expect* more of myself but *do* more from my position in the world.

Purpose
Passion
Progress
People

This book should be viewed as a collection of small pieces I used to find my own way to make a difference—largely finding how to innovate on helping others. I'll admit, the book is less of a solution and more of a series of questions, inspirations, and insights that have helped me discover more about myself and my role in the world. But the framework is where the heart of this book lies.

This is my journey to find purpose, to find where help can be applied, and to do what I believe I was destined to do my whole life: Help people.

MY JOURNEY
So why write a book when I've not found the answers… yet?

In a way, it helps me move down the path. I have many interests and passions, but I feel a call from destiny to help people and to take action at a personal level to address key issues.

I've interviewed key people and learned from experts across the various aspects of technology, connecting fields vital to the success of our start-up. These experts include technologists, psychologists, and computational scientists. Technology is designed to perform a function and achieve an outcome and solve a problem. But some problems are nuanced—how we behave, how we feel, and how we perceive desire.

This led me to a first pass of:

Purpose → Hunger
Passion → Tackling Inequality
Progress → Utilizing Technology
People → Africa

From there, it's enabled me to examine how I can use my skills as an innovator and technologist to drive the most impact.

Throughout this journey, I interviewed key people and learned from experts to understand about passions and the pursuit of purpose, connecting fields involving faith leaders, social justice leaders, nonprofit leaders, and mindfulness leaders. My faith is well-grounded, and my willingness to learn lessons and insights and profound truths from others of different beliefs is broad because the tapestry of humanity is vast and beautifully nuanced. Just like our Creator.

Purposeful living is complex, just as we are, each of us is a combination of spirit, flesh, and intellect.

And in my own quiet, small way, becoming part of a movement is an effort to create a meaningful impact on people around the world.

MY AIMS
Not everyone is ready for major life change—heck, even I am not always sure—so this book will let you find your own path, even if it is to select a nonprofit to volunteer with, a new job that has a social angle, or just a way to be thoughtful about what you hope to do a decade from now.

This book is designed to help you think differently—and hopefully develop your own approach to make your own impact based on your own terms.

Whether you are a technologist who loves technology for its own sake, one of those nerdy developers or coders who know in their heart their work is valued by others, or an academic who never tires of hearing the inquisitive thoughts from students of life who are on a journey of discovery, this book is for those who love to dance like no one is watching and stop to smell the roses. Dreamers of every age will nod in agreement, see their own experiences and ideas on every page, and know their purpose is just around the corner.

This book is a tool for each reader to examine and explore the 4Ps of Innovating on Impact—discovering Purpose, Passion & Progress through People.

Should we expect more of ourselves? Is believing in "happily ever after" so wrong?

Yes, it is fair of me to expect more of myself. And I will do more.

SECTION I:

PURPOSE

CHAPTER 1

BE ALIVE!

The world is very different now. For man holds in his mortal hand, the power to abolish all forms of human poverty and all forms of human life.

—JOHN F. KENNEDY, PRESIDENTIAL INAUGURATION JANUARY 20, 1961

The power mentioned by President Kennedy includes the most critical, the power to find joy for yourself. Joy, your own deep joy, creates a life-giving spring inside you. When cultivated, this spring will overflow, allowing you to share with others.

So, do you know, then, what brings you joy? I find joy in the simplicity of being alive.

Life itself is beautiful—atoms, dolphins, mountains, and nebulae. All inspire and fill me with awe and wonder. And this is where a journey must start.

I set out in 2017, on a journey to uncover the intersection of technology and purpose. To learn from other experts and uncover why I feel such restlessness about poverty, hunger, and inequality. I found I had to come face to face with myself and what brings me joy, which was a foundational step of the journey.

I also found an ugliness in myself. I found that my heart was like a wild onion in the ground, not simply layered but also covered with dirt and hidden underground. I uncovered that, over a full career of working, I lost sight of what is truly important to me, and I substituted accomplishments and comforts. I realized I had spent decades confused. But why?

The answer is complicated.

All my life, my heart burned with two questions: (1) Who am I? and (2) What do I really love?

As an African-American in America, I am a minority. In my deepest heart, I struggled with the inward belief that I was lesser because of my skin color. So I recognized that I had to stay in "my place."

A respected author and speaker from North Carolina, Mr. Larry Winters, has said, "Thou shalt not fool-eth thy self-eth." That was me in my twenties, thirties, and forties. I was confused and fooling myself about myself. I was not honest in my understanding of "who I am." That was the first step of the journey. Understanding, unpacking, and acknowledging the truth of my past. The good, bad, and ugly. You have to know where you are to find your way.

Finding and living truth is the goal. And discovering it has been worth the entire journey.

LOVING LIFE

I was fortunate to have been born in the 1960s because the technology of the time literally kept me alive.

I was born pre-mature and struggled with pneumonia in the first few months of life, I was weak and sick, an incubator baby.

It was a sterile and touch-less environment.

Today they call it attachment disorder, and it may explain difficulties I have suffered all my life. I shrink away from touch automatically, yet I desperately crave touch and love.

Crazy dichotomy, right?

Throughout my life, my mother has told me repeatedly the story of how she prayed for me. So even though I didn't get the constant touch of a mother's loving arms, I did get the constant covering of a mother's loving prayers. And the prayers worked. I lived, thrived, and grew.

I grew up like any other boy, exploring and getting into trouble. I grew up just outside of the city limits in West Texas. My Dad was in the military and we lived on the Air Force Base. In my neighborhood, kids of all colors, shapes, and sizes lived next door to each other and played together in the pool. On the base, we didn't have railroad tracks dividing one side of town from the other. Kids just ran around playing, being ridiculous and loving it.

But I attended school off-base. So even though I had to know "my place" there, I internalized that life on the base was how things should be.

Then my family moved to Anchorage, Alaska while I was in middle school and for the first time, I had a strong enough crush on a girl that I acted.

She was white.

When I professed my feelings for her, she rebuffed me not because I was black but because I was a dorky little kid. She was grown up, a whole year older. Looking back, I guess she was right, because being the dorky little kid that I was, I wrote her a note telling her how much I loved her.

Remarkable mistake!!

I might as well have sent the letter to the six o'clock newsroom because that same day by early evening, EVERY kid in the neighborhood knew what I had written and was laughing at me.

Totally humiliating for a sensitive, love-starved kid. I laugh about it now, but I still think of it as a life lesson: "don't put it in writing." So, I was the star-struck kid. I lived with rose-colored glasses.

I loved life.

THE ENDS AND THEN THE MIDDLE

Do you feel tensions inside, where no one else can see the real you? Do you see that tension as confusion? What is most meaningful to you?

For me, the incongruities in my heart and the first and most important question emerged in the book-ended stories of my grade school and middle school years.

Who am I?

I am the same little boy who believes Jesus is the Christ, God incarnate, born of the virgin Mary, who died for my sins, was raised from the dead, and lives in Heaven with God the Father. I believe the Holy Spirit dwells in us, and that through the leading of the Holy Spirit, the Bible was written. And I believe the Bible is true.

And the Bible says that God created Adam and created Eve and that from the two of them, the entire world's population was born. So, if we are all the same race, the human race, then isn't skin color irrelevant?

So constant tension existed. Who does the Bible say I am, and who does my town's culture say I am?

So, thirty-five years later, after starting a career and family and having visited cultures all over the world, I taught my children the following life lessons so they could live to see another day:

- Cross the street when you can if a white woman is walking alone in your direction.
- Always look away and do everything to demonstrate that you won't be any trouble.
- Remember what I call "Life rule number one" — obey the man with the gun.
- If you are stopped by a police officer, roll down all the windows before the car comes to a stop. Put both hands at the top of the steering wheel and keep your face looking forward until spoken to by the officer. Respond to the officer with "yes, sir" or "yes, ma'am." And most importantly, don't allow anyone in your car to talk back or talk loudly to the officer. Do not ever let anyone in your car who doesn't listen to you in that situation. Their bad behavior means trouble for you.

BEING GROWN UP

Growing up, I learned that a responsible and real man provides for and protects his family, but I began spiraling out of control. I felt if I was capable of working fifty hours, that's what I should do.

In time, I believed *doing* was the goal. What I could attain in terms of resources for my family was the benchmark. I missed the balance between providing for my family and being with them.

But this was not the TRUE start of the problem.

Throughout my military career, I struggled to draw the line between work and the rest of my life. What I did each workday reflected where my heart was inclined.

I experienced ongoing tension. I say I love life and want to enjoy it to the fullest, but the number of hours I spend working each week demonstrates what I truly love. I'm not competing with others to get ahead for promotion; I'm working against myself to get ahead of where I would be if I didn't.

Remember the story of the tortoise and the hare? The tortoise had to keep going and going, slow and plodding to get to the finish line, and that talented hare could sleep and party for hours and its speed allowed it to rapidly reach the finish line.

Everyone in the circles I work in is a hare. They laugh and joke and have fun, and they are so talented they can rapidly reach a goal with ease. I am the tortoise. I am so slow and plodding that I must start early and work consistently long hours just to produce the same goal.

I love reaching the goal.

There is the tension.

FINDING THE CENTER

Do you feel unworthy in some aspect of your life? Is there an activity or passion you cling to that conflicts in your soul with part of your core beliefs? Do you find yourself creating stories around your passion? What defines you?

For me, the battle for my soul has been a difficult challenge to wrestle with. All my adult working life I have struggled with passionate beliefs about how I should live.

I am the high school teenager who asked Jesus Christ into my heart, to be the center of my life. I am the college student who learned Jesus is alive today and wants a personal and intimate relationship with me every day of my life, now and forever. I am the young twenty-something working in the Carolinas who saw, time after time, this same Jesus show up with answers to the deepest and most defining issues.

If I love Jesus Christ and believe He has called me to love and serve Him, why am I afraid to serve Him in ANY capacity that He may cause the Holy Spirit to lead me toward in serving God the Father?

Just because I am the tortoise of the world, doesn't mean I don't like racing. I love accomplishing goals—not for the sake of competing against others but to compete against myself. So should I not do that which I am capable of doing?

I struggle with knowing what I love and acting on it.

Why did I get a master's degree? Why did I seek promotion in my workplace? Why am I involved in a Tech Startup? Why am I serving in my church?

LIVE WHAT YOU BELIEVE
Amid these struggles to understand who I am and what I love, I found inspiration in Kenya on the continent of Africa.

The 15,000 people who lived there appeared to be incredibly hard working. Most mornings when I awoke at 7 a.m., the farmers were already in their fields, digging rows and furrows by hand in the difficult soil—back-breaking work, done without fail or complaint. The people appeared dedicated and resilient but still, they endured hardship.

I met Steve Njenga and his wife Mary there in April 2018, as mentioned previously. I was impressed by the singularity of their focus and purpose: Reduce child malnutrition for the children in the Mt. Eburru villages.

They became missionaries in their home country to help villagers and a people not their own. They endured hardship and poverty from a sense of higher calling. In their work, that focus drives unity, devotion, and purpose.

I learned from Pastor Steve and Mary that each of us has a different destiny.

If you can clearly resolve the tensions and questions you have, work through the confusion, and reach a resolution, should that not lead to action?

Live what you believe and love. Steve and Mary's story addresses my core tensions of who am I and what I love and reminds me of one of my favorite life quotes, by a friend, former Marine Lieutenant Colonel Rocky Ball: "Do right and fear no man."

REFLECTION AND DISCUSSION QUESTIONS
1. Do you know at your core what you love and what brings you joy, deep joy?

2. Have you found the place where you are moved to a life of action, giving deeply of yourself to others?
3. Have you ever struggled to understand yourself? Are you prepared to unveil the various layers of your life so you can move forward?

CHAPTER 2

TO SEE AND TO BE SEEN

The song, "This is Me," was written as an anthemic song for people who had lived in the shadows their entire lives and had stepped into the light, declaring they would be seen and love themselves as they are.

—BENJ PASEK[1]

If you have watched the 2017 movie, *The Greatest Showman* and heard the song, "This is Me," you undoubtedly felt some emotion as the film built up the suspenseful moment as the crew dramatically declared their unique individuality in a moving sing-along. But what resonated deeply within me was the words of the song by Benj Pasek. I felt empathy for the character and the idea the words expressed. I saw in this song my own heart. I secretly joined the chorus, singing loudly within that I too am one of the complicated people living life in the shadows. This is me, marginalized, shut out, and hurt.

---

1 Jenelle Riley. "Behind the Scene: How Pasek and Paul's 'Greatest Showman' Anthem 'This Is Me' Became a Smash Hit." *Variety*, February 21, 2018.

Even if we are not willing to admit it or don't look like it on the outside, each of us is complicated. Inside, we are nuanced and riddled with doubt and guilt.

I have long known about the inner complexity but only recently have I started a journey to reconcile all these stirrings and a growing drumbeat of desire to change. To drop all that I am doing. To fly from the corporate ladder to see a different reality where I can be more uniquely myself, to be seen as I am. As the song says, to declare 'this is me' and trust whatever may come. But inside my own mind, heart, and spirit I am riddled with unworthiness and I rage about it inside.

I have always been, and will always be, just a little boy from Texas. I am not ashamed of always wanting my mother to be proud of me. But I also feel starved for small affirmations. No matter how many times I heard she was proud, that was yesterday. Today, I'm just not sure. It's complicated.

KNOWING WE ARE ALL THE SAME
In college, as part of the Long Blue Line of students of the Air Force Academy, the altitude afforded me the opportunity to occasionally have my head literally in the clouds. In the morning, from the dorm room of Mighty Mach One, the First Squadron of Cadets, I gazed upon the tops of clouds. Each time, I felt like the view confirmed what I believed about being fearfully and wonderfully made.

I believe each person intrinsically has great value and worth. So let me state clearly that I believe the Bible is true.

A few years ago, I read a newspaper article about a lawyer from New York. He worked hard and was very well paid, earning more than $400,000 per year helping high-net-worth clients. However, he felt he was a failure because his friends and classmates were all millionaires with extravagant lifestyles. Since he couldn't live that lifestyle, he decided to take a little more from his clients. He could then begin living the life he felt he should have—until he was caught. He was arrested, tried, and sentenced to jail.

During sentencing, the lawyer was remorseful and tearfully confessed, explaining that his friends and others he respected were more affluent, and he felt he was a failure. He knew that stealing was wrong, but he wanted to keep up with his friends.

So who do you focus on? He focused on those wealthier than he was. So, out of 300 million Americans, he chose to look at the 30,000 who were wealthier rather than the other 299 million who were not as rich as he was. He could not see the 99 percent who were not as well off as he was; he could only see that he was at the bottom of the barrel of the 1 percent.

How do we understand where we fit in the world and decide where to focus? Recent events in my life have caused me to consider that in my own life journey. I joined a non-profit group, watched my father lose his memory, and loved someone in college who never knew. How does it all fit together?

In 2019, I joined the board of a DC-based non-profit, Spero Ministries. The chief aim of the group is to positively impact homelessness in the Georgetown area. I was drawn to the group because of my increasing concern for poverty and hunger. The effort provided a tangible way to increase my understanding of the intricate aspects of hunger and homelessness. It also provided a means to see the people and identify their humanity. To see them as I see myself. One of many human beings. We all need, at some level, to be seen. We are all part of the same struggle and must understand how to purposefully serve one another.

In 2019, I also spent time in Texas with my aging father. We watched sports and movies together. Every once in a while, he'd say, "Will you look at that?" and I'd say, "You know, sometimes that's how it goes.'" My father has dementia, and he no longer knows who I am. I am learning to love my own father in this state of his life where he does not know me.

When he sees me, I'm just some random guy, watching a show and making occasional small talk—very small, because he cannot remember more than just a few seconds at a time. I call it the 30-second memory. We can no longer have a conversation. After one sentence, he does not remember it. So they are one-sentence affirmations.

"Did you see that?" "Why, yes, I did and you're a great guy."

"Isn't that interesting?" "Why, yes, and it's incredible that you saw it, good job!"

At this stage, he mostly is only capable of very small talk. I'm trying to get used to it, trying to accept that it could be ten to fifteen more years like this in declining stages. Like many other families, I am coming to terms with the new reality. But it has also given me a new view of my own mortality. I am thinking of my father and the other twelve residents living in the memory care unit. They are all human beings like me. Reduced capacity but human and deserving of dignity. I saw myself in their shoes. We were all the same.

I see so much of me in their situation. Even when I disappoint myself and waiver in my resolve to live what I believe, I never fully know what anyone else is doing. Like the residents in memory care, I get riled up and confused. I can only think in very small segments. Who will help me find a sense of calm?

Finally, in 1985, while I was in college, I loved a girl who never knew how I felt.

My dorm room window sat 7,258 feet above sea level. From there, I looked down into the Black Forest. On many mornings, the clouds hovered in the forest and I looked down on top of the clouds. It was a romantic scene that contributed to an already romantically inclined heart. But the girl never knew, so it was not really a romance but a dream. In my heart though, I felt like the jilted lover. I was marginalized and overlooked. My perception was my reality.

I lacked love, the specific love from the one person I wanted. I desired that she have the same feelings for me, but it never happened. Even after graduating, the memory of not measuring up still lingers.

These three short examples repeatedly show where my feelings, my heart, and my spirit felt marginalized. I was in the shadows; I found no company. I accepted nothing less than what I believed to be the answer to my pain.

I was alone, mostly in my own mind, even when surrounded by hundreds of people. From the outside, they presumed I was doing well or thriving. But on the inside, I was alone. Regardless of any accomplishment, I felt alone with inner pain. I felt like I did not fit in.

So this is me. Complicated.

BELIEVING WE ARE ALL THE SAME

Have you ever felt complicated?

A jumble of contradictions that no one else knows but you? Neither your parents, your spouse, nor your best friend really knows your inner secrets. I believe it is complicated. We are complicated.

In high school, I began to believe the Bible to be true, and this belief has only deepened. I believe that eternity is real, and Jesus Christ is Lord, and I am not ashamed of this. I will stand before anyone who accuses me and accept any human judgment.

But just as some of the historic figures written about in the Bible show remarkable complexity and seeming contradictions of belief and action, I have lived contradictions in my life. Anyone who knows me well has seen me as a complicated man.

I recently learned from a Bible scholar from Georgetown that eternity is an amazingly long time. From the lens of eternity, what will happen has already happened but not yet. It is the idea of hope expressed in the form of salvation, freely offered by God, who exists in eternity past and eternity future all at the same time. The great I Am. When I accepted the gift of salvation, God already knew every sin I had committed and every sin I would commit in the future, and His offer of salvation was for all of it at one time.

The gift of Jesus Christ is forever, but I am just a mortal. I unpack and recognize one small second, minute, and hour at a time. I feel remorse and sadness when I do not live up to the gift of Christ when I sin anew. I grieve the Holy Spirit and am led to ask forgiveness and confess my daily transgressions and forgive others. That is my daily bread.

So this new understanding of 'already but not yet' became a new lens to understand what has been stirring in my heart about the complicated people we are. Knowing my own defeated state and feeling of unworthiness did not remain just an inwardly focused event. I saw others hurting and I felt moved. I was sparked to action. This is a story of discovery.

My discovery of poverty and hunger has led me to action, but discovering the right activity has not been so easy. I have responsibilities and a family I love and care for, who are part of how decisions are made for my life.

We crave validation one-to-another. We were made to be in relationships. The poor and the hungry desire to be seen in their affliction.

The importance of being seen goes to the very fabric of our being. We crave validation, to be acknowledged in how we were made, in whatever way we choose to express ourselves, the right to make choices about whether to obey God or not. We have uniqueness, just like fingerprints. Some tall, some not. Some brown, some not. Some feel urges, some not. Some born with Down Syndrome, some not. Still, all have value—even when they choose differently. Human value is being, not doing.

It is part of the human condition to want to be in community, but how do we account for differences of opinion? Who recognizes the community of the whole?

What about those who desire to be elite? The fittest. Do you know the popular saying that if everyone is special, then no one is special? Isn't this just the natural extension of the theory of evolution, that justifies the survival of the fittest as being a distinct set apart from the rest?

Does nature allow natural selection to be considered an evolved version of the best? What does it mean if the fittest need to cheat to get that status? Are they smarter for cheating first?

These ideas are contrary to my faith. The Bible says that God created one man and one woman and commanded them to be fruitful and multiply. If literally true, then every human on the planet came from them. Every human, no matter what skin color, size, physical challenges, deformity, or intellect are all the same—made in the image of God. So no matter how we live, no matter how we were born with inner drives, each of us as human beings is to be individually and distinctively validated.

If my father does not recognize me anymore, should I just ignore him, leave him to the nurses of the memory care unit? Let the monthly payments to the nursing staff of the memory care satisfy any family duty or concern. Do I not need to focus on my own life and challenges rather than consider the needs of someone who does not recognize me anymore and will not for however long he lives?

No, I love my father and my mother. I see them.

As I piece together feelings of this most recent experience with my father, being associated with the homeless in Georgetown, and unrequited love in college, I have felt being on the outside and seen the truth. We are all equal, and this part of my journey is my chance to live it. To live as though my father knows me and personally enjoys and connects with each and every visit.

The most important lesson he taught me repeatedly was, "I love you like no one else ever will. I will always love you."

Even with dementia, each of these thirteen residents in the memory care unit is uniquely and individually valuable. We are all human. None should be marginalized.

So this is where I set my foundation. This is where I plant my flag.

I believe I am among the least important people in the world. I am like the ant or the drone bee. I play just a small part of this life, and I am okay with that. I am not the important queen ant nor queen bee. Fifteen years ago, I could not have said that. I wanted to be a somebody.

Today, however, I don't need to be a somebody. I am happy to just be who I am. This is 'Me.'

REFLECTION AND DISCUSSION QUESTIONS
1. Have you admitted to yourself where you have felt hurt? Are you willing to name it?
2. Are you willing to commit to thinking differently, consider that you are part of something bigger?
3. Do you think that you can accept you for you? Are you willing to consider asking for forgiveness? Can you forgive yourself?
4. How does one account for every human on the planet? Are you open to considering that we are all the same? Of innate value and worth?
5. Give $5 to someone homeless on the street and look them directly in the eyes and smile.

CHAPTER 3

FINDING JOY IN SORROW

Two roads diverged in a wood, and I—I took the one less traveled by, and that has made all the difference.
—ROBERT FROST[2]

The last words of Robert Frost's poem express cleanly the concept of choice and consequence. His words also express the conceptual idea of possibility and options. This, I believe, is real freedom.

You are free when you have multiple options and are allowed the right to choose, whatever the situation or circumstance. You are free when there's an arc of possibilities down one path and an arc of possibilities down the other.

---

2   Robert Frost. "The Road Not Taken by Robert Frost." Poetry Foundation. Poetry Foundation. Accessed February 18, 2020.

The last words of the poem are an illustration of life. Along the corridor of hope, doors open to dreams on the one side and opportunities on the other. Choosing is an act filled with joy. The traveler does not have to know outcomes, but by walking through one door, he or she consciously chooses to find pleasant surprises and wonders beyond belief.

I was an African-American living in West Texas in the 1970s, but still, I was a dreamer. And then, in the fifth grade, I was shocked awake from my dream world.

One day, I came home from school crying because a boy named Thaddeus said that my parents "did it" and used his hands to make a crazy gesture. I didn't understand what he was saying, and I told him I was born like Jesus.

I didn't even know what 'being born like Jesus' meant, but I went to Sunday school each week, so my response sounded like the best way to be born. But Thaddeus told me I was stupid, and I literally went home crying. I wanted my parents to reassure me, so the next day I could ignore whatever Thad might say.

Unfortunately, I learned a hard lesson from my dad. He told me about the birds and the bees, and that what I believed was not true. The lesson was not so much about human reproduction but learning that my ten-year-old beliefs were not absolute. There was a reality about the world that would further crash in on my understanding of the world and life. It horrified me.

So you can look at diverging ways to consider how we dream, think, and believe in the world of ideas; differing views make a picture more complete.

I also believe that age changes things. Through the normal sorrows in the cycle of life, a beauty emerges, a sense of understanding and perspective. As a child, I dreamed of the impossible because I did not know anything else. I did not appreciate limitations. I thank my parents for that. I was not told no. I was told maybe, and all I needed was a shot. But now, at fifty-four years old, I dream of the impossible because I believe. I trust in the infinite.

Over time, age provides a larger and larger portfolio of views.

PERCEIVE DIFFERENTLY FROM OTHERS
A portfolio is a collection of material to which you add new material. Each day, we gain new material, new ideas and insights, and new perspectives and lenses through which we view life's circumstances. I think of it like the sands of an hourglass. Sand pours atop one another, creating a mountain of sand. That is a portfolio, a collection of experiences from which you can draw experiences and insights previously not available.

As a child of twelve, the sands of experiences are few, so the perception is limited. At fifty, generally, the experiences are far greater. Understanding action and consequence is more developed. But the sands of experience do not form bricks, and they can be blown around easily. They can shift like the sands in the Sahara Desert. Like the drifting sands of the desert, the sands of experience are beautiful, expansive, and awesome. But I argue, they are also empty. And having a dream fills the land and makes the sands of experience richer and more able to be formed into bricks, which form walls, which form castles, which form cities and nations of opportunity!

I marvel at the dreams of sixteen-year-old Greta Thunberg. Her dreams led to action and have led to millions around the world being energized by the faith of youth to ignite the passion to act. When dreams, action, and attitude can be harnessed together, real and beautiful creation begins.

So the spark that begins a beautiful creation is the act of dreaming. Have a dream. That's it. That's the secret.

Let's have a little thought exercise. For no more than three minutes, consider these three words: "purpose in life."

- What is the meaning of the words? The phrase?
- Can the words be rearranged to better interpret what it means to you?

If you are a visual thinker, what picture comes to mind?

- Do you see volumes of possibilities?
- Do you see a forest of choice?
- Do you see networks of interlocking roads? Hills? Valleys?
- Do you see lights, like blurs swirling together?

If you are more kinesthetic, how do those words make you feel? Are your senses engaged?

- Do they make you feel warm?
- Do they give you a cool and refreshing feeling, like water from a fall pouring over you?
- Do they smell like your favorite memories, cookies in the cookie jar or a pie in the oven?

I find "purpose in life" to be filled with hopefulness. I sense options and see the corridor of hope with incredible doors on either side. At just over fifty years old, my dreams are heavily laced with hope and expectation. To decide to view things with a lens of hope is an act of will. And that hope brings freedom. And freedom makes dreams possible.

REACT DIFFERENTLY FROM OTHERS

I'll share three stories, each separated by roughly ten years, which taught me the lesson of reacting differently.

The most valuable lesson I ever learned was from Michael "Buckeye" Sovacool, a much-beloved leader of a Marine Infantry Battalion in California.

In a meeting, he outlined to the officer in charge of logistics several things that did not meet his expectations and assigned a timeframe to get them fixed. Some of the things included needing paper towels in the bathrooms and painting the signs out in front of the building. Other items were a little more substantive regarding the maintenance of weapons and vehicles, but I only heard the comment about paper towels.

After the meeting, being wise and insightful, he saw the look on my face and pulled me aside to ask if I had questions. So

I asked, "Why were we talking about paper towels?" And his answer changed my understanding of leadership from that moment on. "Brown, how you treat people is how they will act. If you give them a dump to work in and treat them poorly, they will respond and perform poorly. But if you give them a great place to work and treat them great, they will respond and perform great."

Those words hit me like a ton of bricks. It was more than just the golden rule, do unto others as you would have them do unto you. It was the next level. If you give them a dumpy place and environment to work in, they will respond and perform dumpy. If you give them no resources, no paper towels in the bathroom, they will respond by giving no resources to the effort of the team. But if you treat them like they are important to you, if you see their needs as your highest priority and you move heaven and earth to give them what they need, then they will respond and move heaven and earth to accomplish the efforts of the team.

I have never forgotten that lesson.

The next lesson came from my wife's uncle and aunt, Henry "Hank" and Barbara "Bobbie" Smachetti. In April 2004, my wife's father turned eighty years old. It was a major milestone celebration, and her mother orchestrated a surprise birthday bash, inviting friends across the region and family across the country to their place in Wayne, Pennsylvania. Dad was shocked to see so many who had flown in to be with him for his celebration.

Before the birthday boy arrived, Hank and Bobbie arrived. Hank immediately got down on one knee (he was in his eighties), on eye level with my children, and started talking to them. It was one of the most instructive lessons I had ever been given.

I was thirty-nine then and had over fifteen years of working experience. As I watched this man relate to my children, I realized immediately that how you treat people can extend for a lifetime. Seeing eye to eye with people is a way of living, not a management style. That he was bigger, and they were smaller was not the point. Valuing people where they are and accepting them as they are means seeing them where they are. This gives you the credibility that eventually earns you the right to speak into their lives. That's what I saw. That's what I learned.

And immediately I told my wife that his lesson clearly showed me how to be a grandfather. In my heart, I hoped to make him proud one day, seeing that the lessons he taught were understood and passed on. I decided to be the best I could be. I resolved to work at treating people well and seeing people eye-to-eye as a lifetime endeavor.

This was for the long haul.

The next lesson was on May 25, 2018, when I witnessed Aunt Bobbie, a beautiful ninety-one-year-old woman, choose a road that made all the difference. We were gathered in Simsbury for a memorial service to Hank, who had recently passed away. I and others had come to the service brave, somber, and devoted to one another and to Bobbie.

Her name was Barbara, but since college, her friends and family have called her "Bobbie." I had assumed she would be brave and somber for this memorial service, but I was wrong. Bobbie had come to the service resolved to celebrate life. Resolved to live and to fully be alive!

Each of us, in facing death, will have to decide what we believe. Is death the final chapter? How do we enter death's door? Will we enter proclaiming boldly into the night, declaring individual freedom? Will we grit our teeth, thinking we can "will" it away or stubbornly trying to extend for one or two more days, months, or years? Will we go meekly, softly, and with tears, unsure of how it will happen and reluctant to leave the familiar? Will we go eagerly, with anticipation and confidence of a bigger plan, believing death to be the only door allowing us to enter into a greater purpose?

When Hank left this world, he was confident of the next. So, for Bobbie, this was not loss. This event was a celebration of Hank's gain. Hank was more alive now than he has ever been! She believed what he believed!

As we gathered in the hall, I was in the doorway as Bobbie entered. She looked around at the people assembling, and I overheard her ask, "Why did all the young people wear dark colors?" Bobbie was there to celebrate Hank's new life, not mourn his old.

WHAM! Her comment hit me right between the eyes! Hank had taught me that fifty is not the end. I still have a lifetime of treating people well and seeing them for who they are. Now Bobbie was teaching me how we interact and reach other people is not just a management style or a decisive way to act, but it is a decisive way to be. Every facet of how you treat people is connected—this life and the next.

She saw the celebration of new life—the *real* life. We must go through winter to arrive in spring. On the other side, we experience springtime forever, filled with endless opportunity and joy. She believed if you have faith, you will see the LORD and be with Him forever. She expressed this celebration mindset by choosing spring colors for the memorial service: white pants, a pair of lovely open-toe high-heeled shoes, and a light pink blouse with a floral patterned jacket, which had a white background with orange, pink, ruby reds, and flecks of deep purple for occasional leaves.

For her, it was another wonderful day. She demonstrated that she believed and looked forward to seeing Hank again when her time comes to move from winter into spring. She resolved to celebrate life.

I saw what I did not expect, and I was inspired.

This added to my portfolio of views.

REFLECTION AND DISCUSSION QUESTIONS
1. When you have two roads that diverge, is it a choice of better over best, good over bad?
2. How do you perceive the minds and ideas of children? Uninformed? Unrestrained?
3. What do you think about the three words: purpose in life?

4. Do you know yourself? Are you learning more about how you impact and interact with others?
5. Next time you see a child under ten years old, get on one knee, say hello, and ask what their favorite ice cream flavor or dessert is. How did you feel afterward?

CHAPTER 4

DREAM DESPITE THE BUMPS AND BRUISES

For myself, I was a closeted gay man who as a teenager felt like the world was inundating me with messages that you're not good enough or you're unlovable, and what has been amazing about this song, in particular, is you realize the thing that feels like your own private struggle is something that other people relate to when you begin to put it into words.
　　　　　— BENJ PASEK (ABOUT THE SONG "THIS IS ME")[3]

I have spent a lifetime trying to earn a place in the group. I've hoped, dreamed, and wished that others would give me validation that I earned the spot. To get there, I have hidden behind unseen masks.

---

[3] Jenelle Riley. "Behind the Scene: How Pasek and Paul's 'Greatest Showman' Anthem 'This Is Me' Became a Smash Hit." Variety, February 21, 2018.

I hid because of fear. I did not want anyone to see the real me—the sad little me. How many of us wear masks? I'm trying to earn a place, fearing that I will never be awarded one. Gaining achievement after achievement and finding them empty.

Those sentiments are expressed in Benj Pasek's words. His song, performed so powerfully and accompanied visually by a storyline that clearly articulates the felt hurts, is so incredibly moving.

When you become a parent, the full weight of responsibility hits you that your child is 100 percent dependent on you to survive, and it changes you. So as a dad, when I read the words expressing the pain of being a closeted gay man, it deeply moved me uniquely. Because I always tried to protect my children from hurts and pain, I feel a deeper sense of regret that I too could have made a mistake of thinking that safety was on the outside. I too could have made the mistake thinking a safe environment was only the externals and missed the unsafe place inside the child's heart and mind of wanting to be themselves but believing that expressing that outwardly would result in rejection.

I empathize because I too long for validation of place. Parents feel failure when they discover they did not create a safe place for their children to be all they want to be.

CARING DEEPLY IN THE MOST DIFFICULT SPACES

In April 2019, I traveled to Dehradun, India to visit friends. India is an amazing country, enormous and breathtaking in diversity of every kind. It was so much different from every other country I have visited, so much more deeply spiritual than I've ever seen. Just minutes outside the airport, I witnessed a powerfully interesting scene as our taxi driver took us across the river. We passed a large cargo truck being driven by a man who had his eyes closed and hands together in prayer while he drove. When we asked about the safety of the situation, our taxi driver calmly stated that the man must be giving prayers to the water god as he crossed the river and that it was normal.

The beautiful countryside was so varied. In one block, it was metropolitan, developed, growing. In the next block, it was unbelievably depressed, an area of abject poverty. How such first world and third world conditions could all be so incredibly interwoven was remarkable. However, what I noticed the most was the people were all smiling. My takeaway from the whole trip was that people are resilient. They can adapt to their space and find a way to thrive.

The friends we visited are in the health care field, so they worked to bring increased medical services to remote villages and to increase the capacity of basic medical knowledge. Because of the language differences, the medical team received language training, learning the fundamentals of the Hindi language.

We visited the home of the tutor. His wife suffered from multiple sclerosis, and she initially couldn't be introduced to us, but later, when she had the strength, she resolved to say hello. I don't think it was just being hospitable to visitors but a resolve to demonstrate to her family that they were strong enough to endure any pains. She set an example for her family, but it would deeply affect us as well.

We began our visit, having tea, and learning briefly about how the language training was being given. I love languages, so I found it fascinating, but I recognized how intricate the Hindi language is and marveled that the medical team didn't just want to give medicine but also have a good bedside manner and make their patients feel cared for.

The tutor was initially sad that his wife was not feeling well and that they could not all host the short visit with tea and conversation. To everyone's surprise, his wife sent a message that she wanted to visit with us from her bed, where she was being attended by her sister. So we were ushered into her room, where she lay covered with a warm blanket. As we walked in, she smiled, and after a few minutes of talking, she said she wanted to sit up and to wish us well before we left. One member of our group, Nikolas Olivero, a gifted film student from Florida State University, was visibly moved by her gesture and sat beside her and asked to hold her hand as she wished us well.

It was one of the most moving moments I have seen. His demeanor changed, as well as his tone of voice and posture. I could see he was deeply moved by her gesture to sit up and speak to us, even though it caused her great pain, and he empathetically reciprocated.

Feeling the experiences of another (empathy) is powerful. It doesn't always take years of training to gain it; some people move with grace and ease in ways that connect with another.

Being aware of others, truly aware, is one of the greatest measures of maturity.

VULNERABILITY AND NEUROBIOLOGY

In 2017, a wonderful podcast was published in the series called *The School of Greatness*. The episode featured host Lewis Howes, a skilled author, entrepreneur, and former professional football player, interviewing Dr. Brené Brown, national best-selling author of a new book, *Braving the Wilderness*. Dr. Brown is a PhD, a licensed master social worker, and a Research Professor of Social Work at the University of Houston Texas.

This podcast ties in with fear, transparency, hurt, empathy, and rejection. Lewis opened up on the podcast, sharing some vulnerable parts of his youth. He said, "I was always picked on, bullied. And I was sexually abused as a kid by a man I didn't know."[4]

Dr. Brené Brown had spent more than ten years studying vulnerability, shame, worthiness, and courage. I believe at that moment, she saw Lewis not only in her professional capacity but also as a human being. As her empathy kicked in, she responded, "I've learned in my research that in the absence of love and belonging there is always suffering."[5]

The human connection that emerged in that moment was the pivotal lesson to be understood. As Lewis transparently

---

4 "Brené Brown: Create True Belonging and Heal the World." Lewis Howes, February 11, 2020.
5 Ibid.

shared his past hurt, Dr. Brown responded in a way that validated him individually and personally. She saw him, she saw his pain, and she acknowledged it as real.

When my children were very young, they would often get scrapes and bruises while playing, like all children. They would run to Mom or Dad with their booboo. I would kiss their booboo to make it better and ask if they were okay. Most times, after a few tears, a long embrace, and a good Band-Aid, they were ready to go back to playing. This is how I view validation. Sometimes, people don't need the problem fixed, they just need someone to agree with them that the problem hurt them. To give them a little love and attention so they know that everything will be all right. To validate that they have a safe place where they can go when the hurts pile up and are out of control.

When Brené made that human connection, she offered that safe and validating space in acknowledging his hurt. That was the key. Willingness to extend a safe and validating space to someone else. This place of human-to-human communication, sharing, and conveying value allows us to encourage and educate one another.

However, the ability to give and accept human connection may not be so simple an act of will. Understanding yourself may be more complex than it seems at first look. And taking the time to try to understand others may be even more complex.

WOUNDS, UNWORTHINESS, AND THE POWER OF FORGIVENESS

I have discovered that being vulnerable means being transparent, removing the mask. One of my masks covers my fear of being exposed as weak.

I am weak. I have always been weak.

This fear could be the deeper and scientific result of hurts as an infant in the neonatal intensive care unit that impacted my neurobiology. My mentor once shared with me a blind spot that I could not see—low self-esteem.

I now have a better awareness of my self-esteem issues, but I still work hard to mask real challenges. I don't read fast. I move slowly like the tortoise. In some areas, I feel vulnerable in fitting in with the group, wanting to belong but recognizing I don't, and hurting because of what that means. I have goals, but this weakness may be the bottomless canyon that will never allow me to arrive.

The mask allows me to grieve my imperfection in silence, knowing it can never be. Raging at my loss. Yet how can I lose what I could never attain?

When I spend time in the gym, although I do enjoy lifting weights, it in some way gives credibility to my mask. It subtly helps me project strength. Another aspect is the theatrical puffing up of myself to others, showing a false strength to keep people from knowing I am weak, vulnerable, and an easy target. No one wants to be a target. So posers like me try to project strength.

The hardest thing for me, causing so many tears inside, is seeing the strong and confident walk around. Knowing I can never belong. The chasm is so wide. Without saying a word, they know they are strong and fast, they don't have to project. The worst is the occasional conversation and ugly condescending smirk from the strong.

But the understanding of weakness is not all-inclusive but multi-dimensional, and a few things deeply confused me. In 1983, as an impressionable eighteen-year-old, I had just entered the Air Force Academy and participated in the summer basic training course. One day, an instructor guiding the group through an obstacle course told me I was inferior, unworthy of being among the group. He said I would be doing everyone a favor by quitting. I am not sure if his intent was to motivate or demotivate me, but his facial expressions and tone of voice indicated the latter. In my heart, I resolved, "I may not be worthy, and you may have grounds to kick me out, and you may kick me out. But I am not quitting."

I was weak but made my last stand. Over and over the next twenty-four years, I would make many last stands. I felt guilty and my heart hurt, believing my country truly did not care about me. It was confusing to reconcile. I told myself I was unworthy, but I made last stand after last stand.

In 2001, it was a different situation. I was wrongly accused and removed from a leadership role. The team was like a ship with leaks and holes, filling with water. There were many other factors, but, ultimately, "There are no bad teams, just bad leaders."

With my weaknesses on display, I attempted to mask my response while accepting responsibility. I do not like victimhood, so I accept my share of the burden, but my masks kicked into overdrive. I wanted to be vindicated 300 years from now when my great-great-grandchildren uncovered all the documents I saved and exonerated me. However, I was slowly drinking the poison of resentment. The documents I saved were like stinking death pots in my house. Behind my mask, I was suffocating and unaware.

But I believe in Jesus Christ and His death, burial, and resurrection, and I finally decided that if Jesus could forgive me, I, too, could choose forgiveness. I destroyed all my records and forgave everyone involved. Then I forgave myself, for harboring resentment against them for so long, building a catalog of the hurts.

At the end of the interview with Dr. Brown, Lewis Howes shared that he had released the hurt of being molested by removing it from the darkness. He often talked about it, exposing it to the light. The first times were very difficult, but over time, telling of the hurt is easier and less shameful. He eventually removed the stigma of something that was not his fault, but in his mind showed weakness. It is an example to me of the next step in my journey, giving more light to those things and removing the stigma. Ultimately, it is really the forgiveness that matters.

I have a dream and forgiveness and empathy are the doorway. Dreamers walk among us. The dreamer sees life, love, and growth as complex but simple. Dreamers rise above their circumstances because they believe. They see the possibility of a different reality. They see who and what we are, and they believe more is possible.

Let go and move on.

REFLECTION AND DISCUSSION QUESTIONS
1. Do you cover your true self? Are they small masks to make friends or impress a date? Are they big masks, hiding you away from society at large?
2. Are you willing to share hurts from your past, no matter how small or large, to find human connection and validation?
3. Are you willing to believe you are not defined by your own self-doubt?
4. Are you willing to consider forgiveness?
5. Are you a dreamer and look for other dreamers to walk the journey alongside you?

CHAPTER 5

IDEAS, LIKE SEEDS, NEED LOVE TO GROW

———

Your dreams of today will create your future.
—LAILAH GIFTY AKITA

The future is not set in stone, and this is not what Lailah Akita intended to convey. I believe she conveyed the immensity of possibility. Life is filled with dreams and endless possibilities. Dreams are conceived ideas and hope of what can be. So raw ideas matter because they are the stuff of our dreams.

We all have ideas, and we have the courage to let those ideas take root and then share them. Many of us have been taught that some ideas are good and some ideas are not as good, so tons of ideas were decimated, sliced away, and left on the cutting room floor, never to see the light of day. Why? Perhaps the dreamers believed they were not worthy of having good ideas. Maybe they were never taught that every idea fails on the first try. Only in trying again does the refined idea find room to flourish. Sometimes maybe the dreamer picked bad company in which to share and jealousy and covetousness ruled the day, snuffing out hope.

I have an idea that is not based on the desire to become an ultra-billionaire. The goal is to make something worthwhile that will benefit all of mankind. My idea requires a little more science, math, and engineering skill than I have, as it cannot exist without diagrams and formulas, functional engineering plans, and schematics. No scientific person will ever listen to my idea.

What is the truth? Is it genius when someone sees what no one else does and has the bravery to keep declaring it anyway? Is it just dumb luck?

The second law of thermodynamics states that everything tends toward chaos, not order. This applies to the world of ideas and dreams. An idea languishes toward entropy until there is action—sharing an idea, a thought, or hope. Eventually, it becomes a dream, and dreams in action create a future, which is where thoughts, hopes, and dreams collide.

Our bodies are remarkably assembled to rapidly facilitate our ability to quickly develop ideas, thoughts, hopes, and dreams. Dr. Mary "Molly" Potter, a Professor Emeritus of Brain and Cognitive Sciences at the Massachusetts Institute of Technology, describes how the human body transforms to develop thoughts and ideas.

"At high speeds, vision finds concepts, and the brain all day long is trying to understand what it is looking at. The eyes get information into the brain and allow it to think about it rapidly enough to know what you should look at next," she said.[6]

According to Dr. Potter, if the eyes and the brain are finding objects, processing them, determining what to look at next and adjusting the orientation of the head to view the next item, then our minds are flooded with information each minute of the day.

Our eyes find concepts in patterns. Our mind is like an idea bucket and gets filled with conclusions, which are checked against new information and compared to patterns and rapidly categorized. When the mind can rapidly associate patterns to new information, it can process more.

New information our eyes take in every moment of the day is filled with opportunity. See something new and, behold, a new idea can begin to form.

NEW IDEAS

How do you think about the future? Do you see the future as static, well-planned, orchestrated, and designed? I do not believe this line of thinking is the same as "the future is set in stone." Rather, the well-reasoned approach to inputs and outputs suggests if I make these inputs, then in the future, these outputs will occur. Do you see the future as fluid, moving and flowing, rushing with currents and eddies, sometimes pooling, but always with a degree of unpredictability?

---

6   Anne Trafton. "In the Blink of an Eye." MIT News, January 16, 2014.

I see the future as somewhere in the middle. I favor the idea of hope, as expressed by Lailah Akita, in the form of dreams. We find new inspirations, develop new ideas, and unlock the flow toward a new direction, advancing boldly toward an undetermined future like a strong wave that inspiration provides.

So why do you believe what you believe? Did you personally test all the facts? Are there varying perspectives to accommodate? Or did you receive facts or fully formed conclusions from someone else and accept them? What new things have caused you to adjust your thinking?

I have repeatedly discovered that I casually accept conclusions from other people I trust. I have even adopted their conclusions as my own.

I watched my own children grow and saw them develop their own conclusions. I noticed changes when new ideas formed deeply in their minds and hearts. I witnessed some struggles as they uncovered older beliefs, compared them, and then discarded them. That is what we should all do—make decisions for our own lives and form beliefs because we are committed to them. In watching them, I discovered that each of us is very complex but also marvelously unique and individual. I think it is beautiful.

My journey to determining what drives change began in 2017, as I desired something new, but I did not know what. Very early on, I learned something interesting from a noted research scientist, Dr. Brené Brown, a University of Houston Professor of Psychology. She described in a TEDxHouston

Talk her research into connection and belonging. Dr. Brown said, "When you ask people about connection and belonging, they tell you their most excruciating experiences. I ran into excruciating vulnerability." [7]

Her story wove itself into my story because I could see myself in how she described her reactions and feelings. But before we get deeper into the *why*, let's explore the *what* of her statement. What does this say about the future, about ideas, about dreams?

Her topic of connection and belonging obviously seeks to study the relationships of people to people. This talk is extremely relevant to me because my own journey seeks to reconcile a desire to change and my drive to abandon corporate America and jump into the non-profit sector. I wanted to stop thinking about my 401K and think like Mother Teresa.

It seemed to me Dr. Brown had a pre-formed conclusion. Her research was showing her new information about excruciating experiences. Demonstrating excruciating vulnerability to describe connection and belonging did not conform to a pattern she had already believed. When she uncovered excruciating vulnerability as a strength, her conclusions were challenged, and new ideas began forming—that connection and belonging are conjoined with vulnerability and shame. This new idea was like a seed beginning to sprout; a fresh new idea takes root and comes to life with an intensity that cannot be

---

[7] EisseCatherine Wade. "The Power Of Vulnerability | Brené Brown | TED Talks." YouTube video. Aug 7, 2016.

ignored. Dreams are the collection of ideas, thoughts, and hopes; they are hopeful expectations of the future.

A developing idea, like a persistent dream, is wrapped initially by a belief, like the shell of a seed. Like nature, it still requires the right conditions to grow.

NEW GROWTH

What are the right conditions for an idea?

Let's start, as Stephen Covey encouraged, by beginning with the end in mind. How do we get to the future? We reach it one moment at a time. My journey has been to discover something new in alleviating hunger and homelessness by technology. Each step along the way, I discovered new facts, formed new ideas, and wondered about new possibilities. I learned from Dr. Brown that people who live their lives wholeheartedly, which is what I aspire to do, lived with a sense of courage. They were excruciatingly vulnerable. She found those people understood that sharing this vulnerability made them beautiful.

This was an amazing discovery for me. I find delight in new ideas growing and sprouting change. When Dr. Brown found something new, she described it saying, "I want to tell you a piece of my research fundamentally expanded my perceptions. And really it changed the way I live and love and parent."[8]

---

8   "Brené Brown: Create True Belonging and Heal the World." Lewis Howes, February 11, 2020.

To me, her statement is captivating. As I said, I want to live wholeheartedly. I want to give my all, to pour myself out for the sake of a cause, to serve and be counted. I do not seek to be recognized, to be first, or to be important. I feel a sense of importance when I understand and believe that the work I am participating in has value. That is all I need. So when Dr. Brown said that her discovery changed the way she lived, loved, and parented, I stopped.

Clearly, as a successful researcher at the mid-point in her career, she is not prone to whim or fancy. As a mother with children, she has seen more than a few things with her own children and put some of life into perspective, which is difficult to do until you have little lives, little eyes, and little minds you care for round-the-clock. But still, she says the discovery changed her.

She found the water needed to nourish the seed of an idea, to break through its old shell of preconceived patterns and viewpoints. Just like a seed becomes a plant, it started with metamorphosis. The old conclusion cracked, and like a seed began to sprout when the water provided the condition, the new idea became a thought, which will lead to a dream, which becomes your future.

Can you stop for a moment and consider your hardened shells? What do you believe? Do you believe only certain people are smart? Do you believe only certain people can be happy? Do you believe everyone is already happy? Do you believe people express happiness in their own way? Have you honestly stopped to understand what you believe and why?

Life has a common origin, a common starting point. Like beautiful music, it is a created symphony, like a beautifully written sheet of music—in harmony, with intriguing discord, mysteriously melancholy in minor keys but always exciting in treble clef.

I believe that Jesus is the son of God, the Christ, risen from the dead and offering life and salvation to all of us. This belief formed my conviction to the words of the Bible and the understanding of a common origin. As I listened to Dr. Brown, I understood that protecting myself from the strong to shield my many weaknesses from others would never yield opportunities to serve. Only in allowing myself to be vulnerable, in sharing my most guarded secret hurts, could I open windows of blind spots that have emerged in my life over time. My excruciating shame was hidden because of my unwillingness to be vulnerable. Until I could open up, my ultimate goal of serving others would be in jeopardy.

This was new growth. I thought I had been looking for one thing and discovered I was really looking for another. It was the road less traveled. That was my turning point for seeking direction. See guilt not as a wall but as a door to walk through.

FINDING A NEW SAFE IN THE WORLD OF IDEAS

What feels safe to you? Before starting this journey, I felt known and comfortable ideas were the safest and most secure. Now I question the validity of seeking safety and believe growth is a better place to camp out. Seek and find the opportunity to grow. Open to change. Open to what is new. Allow fear of failure to be your partner, not your enemy.

We can infer from what MIT Professor Dr. Molly Potter said about the brain seeking pattern recognition that familiar patterns increase the speed of recognition. This recognition and understanding are the ability of the brain to let the eyes move on to the next thing.

Familiarity equals the feeling of comfort. The comfortable equals feeling safe, and the uncomfortable leads to feeling unsafe.

In the world of ideas, this is how I view what happened for Dr. Brown—the perceived safety of old knowns was gone. She continued her research and found people she interviewed living with their whole heart. They were courageous, living from a place of authenticity. Dr. Brown said, "They had connection as a result of authenticity. They were willing to let go of who others thought they should be in order to be who they were to make connection, and they fully embraced vulnerability. They believed that what made them vulnerable, also made them beautiful." [9]

Her results about shame and vulnerability were not what she expected. Where an anchor point had been anticipated, an unexpected development was discovered.

---

[9] EisseCatherine Wade. "The Power of Vulnerability | Brené Brown | TED Talks." YouTube video. Aug 7, 2016.

The shell of the seed cracked open, and a new idea grew. This is the centerpiece of her story and how I want to challenge you to re-look at your story. Do you have fully formed conclusions? Remember, you are never too old to be challenged. You are never too smart to be challenged.

REFLECTION AND DISCUSSION QUESTIONS
1. Do you allow ideas to challenge what you believe? Are you afraid you may be wrong?
2. Have you considered that fear may be holding you captive?
3. Do you know that new ideas pop into your mind every day based on what you see? Do you limit your surroundings and environment only to one set of stale occurrences?
4. What if you varied your routine and introduced new things over time? Are you worried you might lose your way?
5. What do you believe? Do you fear the future?
6. Did you know most of us are afraid of something? Even the most vocal and strongest are secretly deeply afraid of something, some kind of loss.
7. Are you willing to talk to someone if you are afraid?

CHAPTER 6

I LOST EVERYTHING

Tears shed for another person are not a sign of weakness. They are a sign of a pure heart.

—JOSÉ N. HARRIS[10]

Love comes in many shapes and forms. I have seen it in my own life, as I have greatly loved multiple people and groups.

My life goal is to remember people, not accolades, which has caused people to accuse me of having false humility and incredibly low self-esteem. I don't have many accolades, so maybe that is why I don't really get wrapped around the axle about them. So whenever I get lucky enough to lead any teams, I always work hard to get a picture with the team because I want to remember the people, not any stuff on the walls.

---

10 José N. Harris. *Mi Vida: a Story of Faith, Hope and Love.* (United States: Xlibris Corporation, 2010)

I have mental pictures of people and groups I have loved for over thirty years, and my affection only grows stronger. This is a love story between a young Marine Corps officer and the Marines under his care.

I learned from the experience, and that was the whole point. Learning and training environments create great lessons from great emotions, and it caused me to rethink what was important.

SPACE OVER SPEED

In 1995, I was thirty years old and proud to have been given an assignment as a Company Commander for a group of 177 Marines in the 3rd Battalion, 1st Marine Regiment in California, Company L or Lima Company (called, "Lima Corps"). Lima Company was dubbed as the "mechanized company" because it would eventually be assigned a platoon of Amphibious Assault Vehicles (AAVs) as the ship-to-shore transportation and attack platform. The team was already wildly successful when I joined and had a swagger about them. I was fully prepared to give my life for them and to give myself fully to them and their needs.

The company had been assigned to spend three weeks as part of the opposing force in the Mojave Desert to support an Army training command at Fort Irwin, the home of the National Training Center (NTC) in San Bernardino County, California. One purpose of the NTC is to help Army war-fighting brigades become better prepared to fight and win the nation's land battles. The chance to work at Fort Irwin with the Army's 11th Armored Cavalry Regiment as the

Opposing Force (OPFOR) gave us the opportunity to work and think like a mechanized infantry team and perform maneuvers using a laser tag-like system to simulate force-on-force operations in short duration during 100 percent full-speed exercise events.

Even better, the construct of the exercises gave both sides, the "Blue Force" and the OPFOR, a chance to "fight" mechanized battles with a real thinking enemy—a chance to act-react-and-counteract in a real battle situation.

It was brilliant and beautiful.

Lima Company was the OPFOR's light infantry asset. In a largely mechanized force engagement, a small company-sized light infantry unit actually might create a quirky challenge. The training is intended to make the Army Brigade, the Blue Force, better and more prepared for future operations. Little quirky challenges help commanders become better. That is why the Army NTC asked the Marine Corps for the help.

As the light infantry operating in a mechanized world, unlike the rest of the OPFOR team, we were actually unconstrained. The OPFOR mechanized forces had specific doctrinal tactics to follow, including how they could react when situations started evolving. We had none of those restrictions. For us, it was like operating in a real environment.

The total exercise would last five days in the field, arranged into three battles. Each battle would be constrained to roughly thirty-six hours of play and had a broad, overarching scope, and the OPFOR was constrained by a discoverable

OPFOR doctrine. The two sides were given roughly six hours to get into a starting position, and then the Blue Force was given roughly twelve hours to initiate a plan to conduct surveillance. When the thirty-six-hour clock started, enough time had elapsed that both sides would use their assigned assets to discern how the other side could impact their ability to perform the assigned battle task.

For my team, five days in the field in three separate types of engagement, one attack and two defenses, was a challenge. Because of the length of the time in the field, one challenge was logistical support for the people and equipment in an always-hostile environment. Though we had exercise breaks during the hot wash sessions, everything else outside of those three-hour periods was always hostile because we could be under surveillance by the "enemy" at any time.

How and when do we get more water? Ammunition? Fuel? Food? Batteries? How do we discard refuse?

All of that was a real consideration.

Our first battle was an attack.

The OPFOR Battalion Commander provided a battle brief for all the company commanders. The light infantry mission was to destroy the outpost and emplace a direct fire weapon, powerful enough to provide significant supporting arms fire for the OPFOR mechanized team. This system would allow the main OPFOR attack to approach unimpeded.

Since the light infantry team was not expected, my company planned a fairly simple mountaintop approach and assault on the outpost. I expected a mechanized team of four to five vehicles at this outpost, and we would descend on this outpost on the desert floor. I didn't think anyone expected us to approach over the tops of the hills.

We started the movement at twilight. The company was scattered over a kilometer and a half to make this night assault. I had led teams in forested climates, but the desert setting was a new one for me. I was trying something I thought novel—using a tracking sensor for my team of assault men to let the infrared sensors of the DRAGON's anti-tank spotting scope give the team a night sighting system on the mechanized vehicles in the outpost as we approached. After five hours, we crested the final ridgeline into what I assumed would be our final coordination point to deploy into our attack formation.

I will never forget those final moments descending that hill.

As we scaled down that rocky hillside, strung out across hundreds of yards, we were unaware that immediately in front of us on the desert floor sat a cold Bradley Fighting Vehicle. It had been there for hours, putting off no heat signature, and in it sat a Blue Force team with their advanced optics, watching us easy prey unwittingly walk into an ambush.

I can still see the flashing lights of the Bradley's simulated gunfire. I can still hear the firing of my team's infantry rifles and the shouts of Marines reacting to being fired upon. It was the first time I realized I would have to personally fight to survive. I went from leading the team to firing my own weapon in an individual fight to the death.

That fight lasted an hour as we scrambled down the hillside and across that desert floor. With the morning light and the help of OPFOR supporting fire, the Blue Force Bradley Fighting Vehicle was destroyed, and what remaining force I had reached the outpost area to find nothing there.

My team of 177 had been reduced to ten to fifteen survivors, including me.

NO WAY! IT DOESN'T WORK?
The fight took a toll, but the real sobriety was in realizing who was and who was not still alive.

Your buddies, your brothers-in-arms—some seriously injured, many dead. As the light started showing that carnage to the ten to fifteen of us still alive, the psychological impact was immediate.

In that harrowing moment, I knew the assault was only half of the mission. The other half was emplacing the direct fire weapon so the rest of the OPFOR Battalion could have a fighting chance. We had to get the weapon into place on the newly captured high ground.

What was left of the team was exhausted and demoralized, but the mission had to be completed. That assault weapon wouldn't walk itself there, and the weapons' bearer was dead.

So I picked up the heavy weapon system, put it on my shoulders, and started up the hill.

A few minutes later, I looked back and saw the few remaining members of my team who could still move following me up the hill carrying the tripod and ammunition.

At the time, I was just glad someone had the other parts and I didn't have to make round trips to get everything up there. I was also proud of them—we were working together to get the job done.

I now know it was one of the purest moments of team love I ever encountered.

As we reached the top of the hill to set up the cannon, I looked over the ridgeline and saw a four-person crew from the Blue Force team with a small jeep. They were unaware of our presence, and it was obvious they were in the middle of waking up, making coffee and breakfast.

I quickly put the few of us there into a position to attack. I had one or two of the Marines with rifles move to the flank so we could attack and destroy this team. Clearly, we had the element of surprise, though we were wearied from the battle a few hours before.

As I mentioned, this training event used a laser tag-type system, and as we assaulted their position, a group of exercise controllers raced to our position and started sorting out what was happening. The controllers determined the skirmish to be a victory for my small OPFOR team, so we quickly returned to the cannon to get it operational.

After all of that, the weapon did not work.

It was a total failure.

FAILURE AND VICTORY
In the dawn hours on that desert hilltop, my mind raced with lessons learned—all of them, "Failure, failure, failure."

I had failed my team. I had not done enough to position or provide supporting fires. I had not created enough intelligence space for us to have found that Bradley Fighting Vehicle before it pummeled us. I had not caused that cannon to be double-checked or triple-checked to know it would function when the time came. I was concerned about having embarrassed the Marine Corps. They sent my company all the way here and I had disappointed everyone.

An hour later, one of my leaders and I went to the first battle debriefing with the controller referees.

The ride to the debriefing site was the longest ride I've ever endured, knowing I would be walking into a session of public humiliation. I was ready but reluctant to accept public repudiation for failing to accomplish the mission and to be held personally accountable.

To my surprise, the rest of the OPFOR team cheered! There were congratulations all around, back-slapping, and handshakes.

It was remarkably unsettling.

It would be another fifteen minutes, when we were deep into the controller debriefing before I learned what had actually happened.

It turned out most of what had happened the night before and in the early morning was insignificant. The result, however, was that it put my team in a location completely unexpected by the Blue Force. On the top of the hill, what had seemed a relatively insignificant and small firefight with the crew making coffee was the turning point of the entire battle. The crew on the mountaintop was the main Blue Force coordinating function and technology outpost. The loss of that crew completely removed the battle coordination capability for their entire brigade team.

Without over-watching technology, the Blue Force team was operating completely in the dark. They were helpless against the OPFOR advancing attack. Our OPFOR battalion team had rapidly and easily destroyed the Blue Force's command and control structures and picked off their team one by one.

Actually, what I had considered deep and utter failure was the turning point leading to victory.

It shaped the way I would think for the next twenty-five years.

HOW DO YOU MEASURE FAILURE?

Is it okay to feel the pain of failure? Is it okay to doubt yourself? Is it okay to be afraid of ridicule in the face of failure? Is it okay to be ready to accept blame?

Is it okay to give a little more when you are tired? Is it okay not to know if anyone will follow you or if anyone is really left? Is it okay to be surprised that you actually won?

CHAPTER 7

WE MUST DO SOMETHING

The hopes for the future of the people in the world I know is plummeting, dramatically.

—AUDREY EWING[11]

How many of us really have a perspective of what hope is, as Audrey Ewing describes? The meaning of hope and future came crashing down on me in November 2019, when a close friend had a stroke and was hospitalized. This has caused me to reflect upon my own life and how fragile I am. But what I see as fragile and fleeting is the opportunity to have an impact.

I did not know as a twenty-year-old that life would be more complicated as a fifty-year-old. But when I turned fifty, things

---

11 Audrey Ewing. "Think Millennials Have Issues? Just Wait for Gen Z." January 10, 2019.

become a little more complicated. I discovered that being an encouraging parent of kids who were twenty-three and twenty-one was not so simple. While I thought I was sharing my views from a safe place, their views were opposite in perspective. I'm having to learn to keep my mouth closed more often, to make space for their ideas to be expressed. Setting firm boundaries but still allowing their new perspectives to be heard.

I did not know my father would become stricken with dementia and no longer recognize me. Seeing him that way does have an impact. I love him just as he is, but he doesn't recognize that anymore, so now it's about doing what is right without reciprocation. It is all tricky.

I desire to help the team on my job grow beyond where they are today. I see a path to get to the next level, but I'm frustrated that so many of my ideas seem clear enough to me, but not to my co-workers, who look at me like I'm from another planet. How many times should I experience this before I seriously consider reevaluating my ideas? The whole world can't be wrong, so isn't there a point when I have to say, "Maybe I'm wrong?" A co-worker said I'm like the high school football quarterback, who constantly comes up with these complicated, tricky plays that never work—of course, until it does.

So, in light of my friend's health challenges, I better appreciate that I will never be twenty years old again and I will never be fifty years old again. Those ages are history. But I don't have to roll over and play dead just because I'm getting older and challenges are all around me. I want to live for another seventy-two years, so I have so much ahead of me to be discovered.

One day I will die. I have already decided where I want to be buried and the non-descript method that I want any marker to have for my burial place. I've drafted a memorial program and have some instructions about the thirty-minute service I want. Let's have some cake, some colorful balloons, and dance just a little and then move on. At that time, I will actually be more alive than I had ever been here on Earth!

INSPIRE YOURSELF
Let's get focused here.

What does it mean to be alive? According to Audrey Ewing, the hope of the people is plummeting. How do you reconcile what you think it means to be alive and what Audrey Ewing is saying? Do you agree with her assessment? Do you see climate change and feel remorse or sadness? Can her statement be looked at from a nuanced perspective?

I have a nuanced perspective. In one aspect I agree with her, but from another perspective, I do not. Until a week ago, my view of climate change was complicated. Now, with scientific discoveries of volcanic activities under the glaciers of Antarctica, I have a totally different perspective. The shell of older conclusions has cracked, and new ideas are growing.

Audrey Ewing mentions "hopes," "future," and "I know" and ties them to the idea of plummeting, forming a picture of despair. But in that despair, we find the opportunity to change. From rock bottom, the only way is up, so her words are a spark for eternal optimism filled with possibilities.

I believe eternity exists. In high school math, one of my favorite concepts was the asymptote. The line which described the approach of a curve, whose distance extended to infinity. I believe in infinity and in eternity. With this perspective, the fundamental idea that anyone can truly know the world is an infinite problem to solve. Any human can only see, at best, a 165-degree field of vision. No human can naturally see behind them, so knowing this world is an expression of perspectives.

If eternity exists and not all input is seen by one person, then what may seem like an end to one person could be a beginning for another person. In January 2020, I am naturally getting older every day and discovering new facts. If I can change my perspective, then others can also change their understanding. Here the words 'I know' are the actual challenge. What do they mean?

I'd like to share the parable of the cracked pot:

> A potter was speaking to one of his clay pots. The pot was older and upset. It felt downtrodden and despised being old, misshapen, and riddled with holes. It considered itself a malformed creation.
>
> The pot compared itself to the beautiful pots. They were well made and sold for good sums.

No one had ever considered the old pot for purchase.

The potter picked up the pot, along with a few others, and traveled to the well for daily water. All the pots were filled with water, placed on a cart, and carried back toward the potter's home. The pot put every effort into holding its water, but because of the holes, the water leaked away before they reached the potter's house.

The pot fell into despair and cried aloud at its failure.

The potter picked up the pot and asked, "What is wrong?"

He learned the long story of failure felt by his creation. With compassion in his eyes, the potter lifted the pot and turned it to see the journey they had just taken from the well to the house. "Look back along our walk," said the potter. "What do you see?"

"I just see a long dusty road with flowers on one side," said the sobbing pot through sniffling sounds.

The potter replied, "How do you think those flowers came to bloom? When we walk to the house each day, the ground receives water and helps them to grow, because you pass by."

What the pot felt was a defect was actually a beautifully purposeful design.

The parable of the cracked pot is about how we see ourselves. The moral of this story is that we should accept ourselves and believe we are contributing to the world in our own little way. We can inspire ourselves if we take the time to value ourselves for who we are. Our lives contribute to beauty, and its results are right in front of our eyes. If we just turn our heads a small degree, we will see where each of us inspires something in others and that should inspire us. Can you see yourself in this story?

No value, no inspiration. Know value, know inspiration.

INSPIRE A TEAM
In 2003, I was drawn to McLean Bible Church, which I felt was comprised of people who shared my faith and belief in Jesus as the Christ. The early 2000s were filled with trying to understand 'terrorism' in the post-9/11 world. It was a time when we were engaged in the so-called War On Terror, and there was tremendous moral confusion.

During this time, a young teaching pastor named Dr. Todd Philips led a group of twenty-somethings in a ministry called Front Line in Washington DC during the late 1990s and the 2000s, so there was always a buzz within the group. As some aged into their thirties and left, others came, so there was always a fresh crop of young professionals gathering to spend time together.

Dr. Todd Phillips was a respected Bible scholar. The group of mover and shaker twenties he led was identifiably, as a generation, unified in resolve. They believed they would be the next greatest generation. In an interview, Todd stated, "In 2007, we went as a group and watched the movie *Amazing Grace* about William Wilberforce. After, they came and said, we want to make a Wilberforce moment. We want to do something."

This is an example of how Audrey Ewing's words suggested the hope of the people is plummeting, but this group of people saw opportunity abounding and had the spark and strength of passion to do something new.

After much research, they decided to impact Liberia within twelve years. A great awakening had been stirred, and in 2008, this group moved to establish a non-profit, The Last Well, with the mission to bring sustainable and drinkable water to every part of Liberia by 2020.

This is an example of the infinite, of eternity. These believers were asking God to honor their prayers, to bring about a change in the poorest of countries, to bring sustainable and clean drinking water where it didn't currently exist—in every part of Liberia. It seemed impossible.

In 2017, The Last Well needed over $700,000 to meet its goals, and in 2018, they needed over $500,000. In September 2019, of the 4,000 communities in Liberia, The Last Well, Inc. has reached over 2,500 communities. In this last stretch, with the hardest geographic sites to be reached, it has been miraculous to achieve.

This is what it means to inspire a generation, to inspire a team. Find a cause worth giving your life and dedicating your talent and treasure to see it completed. What about you? Will you give to The Last Well?

Finally, do you see the greater good that you and your generation offer to the world? You can move mountains together. Even if you are ninety-five years old, your generation has gifts and talents that will inspire others. Time doesn't determine how much one can inspire in others—heart is what makes others want to join in your cause.

A young man in Tiananmen Square, by himself, silently faced off with a line of tanks and brought them to a halt. Riveting and inspiring for millions across the world, he inspired a generation.

You can too.

REFLECTION AND DISCUSSION QUESTIONS
1. Do you have hope in the future?
2. Do you see your actions as significant or insignificant? How do you inspire yourself?
3. What teams are you a part of? Family team? Work team? Volunteer team? Do they inspire you? How do you inspire them?
4. What is your Wilberforce Moment?
5. Will you give to bring clean and drinkable water to all of Liberia? www.thelastwell.org

CHAPTER 8

IT IS THE PEOPLE, NOT THE POSITION

You can either see yourself as a wave in the ocean or you can see yourself as the ocean.

—OPRAH WINFREY[12]

The ocean is vast, and Oprah Winfrey's words prompt you to ask, "Do I see the waters as lifeless or filled with life?" Some see the ocean as cold, deep, and formidable, others as unforgiving and powerful. Some may see the ocean as warm, wide, and teeming with life. And a few may see the ocean as mysterious and ancient. Those few will be more focused on the creatures in the depths, undisturbed by human presence since life in the seas began.

---

12 NDTV. "Full Transcript: In Conversation with Oprah Winfrey." NDTV.com, January 23, 2012.

The ocean is alive and filled with life. In part, I see the infinite possibilities in the vastness of the seas because I have traveled the ocean several times. After spending three weeks without seeing land, you gain a different perspective. Oprah Winfrey's words question the perspective of being a wave or being the ocean. Is your perspective that of being tossed around on the surface like a wave or is your perspective about being stable and resilient?

If you view yourself as an ocean, it diminishes the opposite mindset of victimhood, which is being tossed around like a wave. It is a question of how we react. Victimhood suggests having no power. Everything that happens is because 'they' willed it to be so. Victimhood is an excuse to cover behavior that knowingly violates other people's rights.

Every human on the planet has intrinsic value because they are created in the image of the immutable God. So everyone on the planet has a valuable opinion, and no one should be completely discounted. We don't have to all agree but should find a way to be respectful of each other's right to one's own ideas and thoughts.

It can be difficult accepting that others have the right to their own ideas or even accepting ourselves when we have conflicting ideas.

Sometimes, we do not live up to our own expectations of ourselves. This is embarrassing to admit—I love people, but sometimes in the heat of a disagreement, I have stopped liking someone. The issue caused me to cease seeing the human.

Although complicated, destiny is not determined by such singular mistakes. You can get up again and try to do better. That is having a deeper character, like the ocean. Keep trying to be a better person. Live for others.

SEE PEOPLE NOT ISSUES

When I was a teenager in the 1970s, Russia plus several others formed a union of communist soviet countries called the Soviet Union. The country had its origins just before World War II, and it was powerful. After the nuclear arms race in the 1950s and 1960s, the threat of nuclear war between the United States and the Soviet Union was a real possibility. The era was called the Cold War, and as a teenager, I was part of a society living with fear all the time.

Here's why I thought of the Cold War often as a teenage boy.

The merit badge system requires a Cub Scout to perform activities and either a parent or the Scoutmaster then signs a form, attesting to the completion of the activity. Around the fourth grade, in Abilene, Texas, I had learned to write in cursive. During Vietnam, my father was often deployed away from home. So for the first merit badge requirements, I used my newfound skills and signed my mother's name in cursive. At the time, I assumed I was on the way to the top. But the Scoutmaster did not respond well to my forgery skills, and my scouting career ended abruptly.

By the time I was a teenager, we lived in Anchorage, Alaska. I played baseball on the local team and played saxophone in the middle school band. But I wanted more activities, so I asked to join the Civil Air Patrol (CAP) and became a cadet airman. I dreamed of flying and loved the idea of wearing a uniform. Fortunately for me, CAP and Scouts weren't connected, so my career as a forger would not follow me. I had a chance at a fresh start.

I was also a nerdy kid. I loved movies, playing chess, and dreaming of being a famous saxophone player. But I also loved being in the CAP, and one of my favorite learning modules was about how we could be helpful in the event of a nuclear war. We learned about the different types of radiation, the difference between the types of nuclear weapons detonations, and how one type or another produced differing radiation emissions. In the CAP, we could be part of radiological detection teams. So I learned about and memorized the half-life duration and effects of gamma and beta radiation. I learned about nuclear fallout and radiation sickness.

I learned how, even in the worst of times, I could learn a skill that would allow me to help others.

But the 1970s was also a challenging time for a young African-American boy. I was especially sensitive to the environment, and even though my parents did a fantastic job of shielding me, I had no sense of worth about my skin color and who I was. I have had to work through this struggle my entire life, reconciling how I see myself. While I had a core set of faith-based beliefs and a sense of my own level of competence, I also saw subtle clues that my skin color really defined my worth. So, as I learned about being helpful in the event of a nuclear attack, I wondered if I were a survivor and I passed a white survivor on the street, would they say hello?

Or, even as one of a few nuclear survivors, would they ignore me because of my skin color?

The conflict was not this issue but my own interaction and tolerance. I had my own demons of discrimination. One of the adult leaders for the CAP squadron was a member of the Army Base Fire Department, and something about him always rubbed me the wrong way. Even though he was trying to help kids, I disliked him and thought he was thick-headed and slow. Whenever I saw him, under my breath I would call him "fat dummy." I was in conflict with my own character. I hoped to be seen and acknowledged, but I did not value this man and associated only negative thoughts with him.

In November 2018, I walked the streets of Georgetown, in DC. The sky was beautifully clear. As I walked around, I noticed a place in the park where it looked like six black plastic bags were sitting, and I thought to myself that these might belong to one of the several homeless people I had passed on the streets of Georgetown. The thought took me back to when I was a teenager, wanting to be seen and acknowledged but a human with clearly conflicted character.

The crisp mid-morning temperature was perfect sweater weather, and the brilliance of the sunny day made the slight chill in the air almost a picture-perfect example of the changing seasons. The sunlight shimmered across the Potomac River, near the stretch alongside Water Street, with Rosslyn in Arlington on one side and Georgetown on the other.

In this moment, I came face to face with my conflicted character. I only saw plastic bags in front of me, but my mind was racing up the ladder of inference, creating a story of how they got there. I imagined someone homeless, attempting to protect their possessions from weather. As the story solidified in my mind, my conscience called me to see the possibility of people and not the issue. I had lost sight of the people. In my buzzing mind of fabricated ideas, I dropped my natural inclination toward compassion to take up the picket signs and protest poverty, seeking credit for trying.

Selfishness. That was what my conscience suggested to me. Selfishness caused me to look for a way to puff myself up. All around me were other people, carrying on with their daily lives. How had I compassionately considered them and prayed for them to enjoy this beautiful day and the one who made it? I was challenged by my own character, and like the wave, I was tossed about in imagined ideas.

I had failed again, but failure was not the end of the story. My conscience called me out, and with forgiveness, I stopped, turned, and started anew to try being better. In time, I hope to demonstrate I learned my lesson. That is what it means to get up again.

CARING FOR PEOPLE

The exact opposite of selfishness is generous giving, which manifests itself in passion to be with and care for others. When passion is nurtured over a long period, it becomes deeply rooted, a part of our identity.

I discovered this depth of passion during an interview in July 2018, with Massoma Alam, author, speaker, and philanthropist. Massoma graduated from the University of Buffalo with a Bachelor of Science in Biology and Psychology and her master's degree from the University of Chicago School of Psychology. She had dreamed of being a doctor as a child, being a part of a family identity, and went to medical school fueled with a purpose to achieve her dreams. She said of this time in her life, "I studied for this for a really long time."

Massoma Alam was confronted with her character as soon as she entered medical school. Would she be like the wave, tossed around to fulfill what she presumed was her purpose to be a doctor and live her family identity, or would she be like the ocean, warm, wide, and driven by her passion for life? For us, on the outside looking in, isn't it just a first-world problem between awesome and amazing? That is the real question I was on a journey to uncover, seeking the expertise she offered.

The question Oprah posed, about being the wave or being the ocean, is not a first-world problem. Every human on the planet wrestles and works with it. In 2018 and 2019, I traveled the world, searching to test the words of Massoma Alam, to find people, passion, and purpose. I visited Nairobi, Kenya; and Trier, Germany; and Dehradun, India; and Akureyri, Iceland. I sought to find the answer to the condition of passion in the human heart. Does your style, standard, and station in life determine who is tossed about like the wave or who is steady and stable like the ocean? Does your ethnicity, nationality, gender identity, or affluence decide who succumbs and who gets back up to try and try again?

I observed that human beings of all kinds struggled with the same things—to be a victim or to recognize the ability to respond. Stephen Covey proposed the idea that response-ability makes us all the same. Though some have a more difficult road in their choice, we can all choose. Even in the most difficult situations like being held against our will, the choice still exists. Will we be like the wave or the ocean?

Massoma Alam felt a purpose to be a physician but a passion to help people. Despite the strong sense of purpose driving her successes, in medical school, anxiety began to manifest. She completed the first year in medical school, allowing her willpower to control her concentration. She focused on studies and continued diligently on her way to becoming a doctor. In the second year of medical school, when she began doing clinical rounds with other students in the teaching hospital, her deep passion for people became more evident. Although she was living her dream of being a physician, she came face to face with the storms of her passion. Medical students are taught to avoid emotional attachment to patient cases. Clinically observe, assess, make medical determinations based on experience and symptoms—that is the professional standard for physicians. It was the expected behavior of medical students. But when Massoma saw the people's emotional pain, she could not distance the people, their pain, and her passion to help.

Massoma said, "I remember some patients, though sick, asking to be discharged, saying I have to go into work because if I don't, my wife won't get paid."[13] She faced a conflict of

---

13   Massoma Alam, interview by author, July 17, 2018.

character. On one hand, she was on the cusp of entering into what she thought was her purpose, to become a doctor, but on the other, the depth of her passion to help people weighed heavy. To have achieved so much, yet have so many boundaries and social expectations weighing, like the winds blowing the tempest tops of the waves, was a real struggle. Would she stay the course, get her medical license, begin her practice seeing patients, all the while suppressing the depth of her inner self, or was a viable alternative available? Massoma Alam chose what Oprah Winfrey called being like the ocean. Warm, wide, and filled with passion, she chose real people with real problems and real emotions, and she walked away from medical school.

SEEING AND SERVING
Massoma Alam's mature understanding of her passions might have more easily allowed her to stand for truth. Her truth. Her true passion was helping people, not stoic clinical practice.

So I've learned to start here, with people. Massoma Alam's passion for helping people woke her up at night; for you, it may be something completely different. Like the plastic bags in the park and all the people walking around on a sunny day, don't be lost on the ladder of inference, making up stories with nonexistent facts. Take what you see in front of you and begin serving there. Allow what sparks a passion within you to become the goalpost upon which you set your sights. Passion drives focus, which ultimately yields results. It might not be on your watch or in your lifetime, but passion prevails. Passion results ultimately in beauty, in creation, and defines a destiny—a spark that brings life.

Merriam-Webster defines passion as emotion, "intense, driving, or overmastering feeling or conviction" or "an object of desire or deep interest."[14] The awakened spirit longs and, like a geyser, erupts with power and sheer kinetic energy. For the passionate, there will always only be a declarative statement. "Ah, yes, there it is!" Passion helps make you alive.

Be passionate for connection, passionate for people, because we are all related and, in fact, one race—the human race.

REFLECTION AND DISCUSSION QUESTIONS
1. Do winds of adversity rule your life? Have you considered your ability to respond differently?
2. Have you ever felt a conflict of character?
3. Is failure permanent? Am I always a failure if I fail just one time? Is it like an incurable disease or a destiny? How many times can we fail and still be able to try again?
4. Have you ever struggled with self-image? Are you willing to seek help and support?
5. Are you passionate about something? Did you know that your passions will change over time and that you can celebrate the new ones?
6. What is your purpose and what are your passions? Are they the same thing? If not, what will you do about it?

---

14 "Passion." Merriam-Webster. Merriam-Webster. Accessed February 18, 2020.

SECTION II:

PASSION

CHAPTER 9

FINDING PURPOSE AT CAMP

Greater love has no one than this, that someone lay down his life for his friends.

—JOHN 15:13 (ESV)

These words, spoken over 2,000 years ago by Jesus, are true and filled with rich context on many levels theologically and practically. As I started my journey to understand what I should be doing and where I could add value, these words provided guard rails for me. The central point is not self-focused but other-focused. Getting out of the way of myself and considering others as more important is central to the idea.

The previous chapters discussed ideas and lessons learned on the journey I started in November 2017—to find a way to incorporate my technology focus with a growing passion to address hunger and poverty in the world, to see and serve a cause addressing inequity, injustice, and vastly different conditions people around the world endure. I wanted to connect the 4 P's—people, purpose, passion, and progress—in a way that would bring me peace in deciding to step boldly into a new phase of life.

I suspected that my ladder of life's work was leaning against the wrong building. Do I keep climbing the ladder, hoping to somehow attain more success like my colleagues, classmates, and friends who are more successful than I am? Do I somehow keep climbing this ladder in hopes that it reaches a plateau that I can then use as a megaphone to call attention to the conditions of human beings in our world of 2020—without a secure source of food, shelter, or emotional solace?

I know I can't solve all the world's ills. I do not seek to solve poverty once and for all; that is not within anyone's power. But I do believe I can help someone else every day until my last breath. A little boy on the beach tossing starfish back into the ocean doesn't worry that he cannot get the thousands of starfish on the beach the relief so desperately needed, but he can help one at a time, consistently, for as long as he has the breath to help. Whether anyone joins him or not, he can be diligent and faithful with no fanfare—not seeking his own book deal and movie rights, not seeking a speaking tour and fame. His passion and purpose were solely to help others. That is what I seek—clarity.

The path to self-discovery is a journey. I have arrived at this idea based on the words of two wise yet radically different people who spoke about being lost and finding your way. The first was spoken by Captain Sam Tangredi of the *USS Harpers Ferry* to a group of U.S. Navy officers. He said, "When you have lost your navigation aids, come to all stop, figure out where you are, and then get underway." The second was spoken by Rear Admiral Ron Hewitt, U.S. Coast Guard to a senior leadership group. He said, "It's not about the destination, it's about the journey."

My takeaway was that knowing the destination is vital, but how you get there is important.

HEARING

Having navigation aids is crucial, and as my captain taught me in 1997, the lesson still applies today in 2020, in ways unrelated to guiding a small boat in dark and fog-covered waters. A navigation aid is a fixed reference point on a map that can help chart a course in the waters. By periodically checking the current course with the expected location of the navigation aid, a true course can be discovered.

My own journey to uncover purpose was like coming to an all stop. In 2016, while our firstborn child was in college, I told my wife I was uneasy about my purpose as a full-time employee. As I mentioned previously, after hearing Charles Swindoll give an analogy about poverty, I immediately reoriented my thinking, talents, skills, and desire to make a difference. We did not agree about my leaving full-time work but set an appointment to have a family meeting. At 1:30 p.m. on June 1, 2020, we'd discuss leaving corporate work to start a new chapter together in the non-profit sector. We stopped forward motion to find navigation aids. I needed to understand where I was before I could get underway.

I discovered research by Paul A. O'Keefe, Carol Dweck, and Greg Walton. The research, published in the scientific journal, *Psychological Science*, found that people have one of two mindsets about new interests. One mindset, called a fixed mindset of interest, involves people waiting to be found. The other mindset, called the growth mindset of interest, involves people developing, through commitment and investment, and achieving new growth. I considered what these could mean for me, working to understand the passion I felt for change.

The three researchers shared that "innovation requires both reaching across fields and maintain that interest even when the material becomes complex and challenging. A growth mindset of interest may help promote this kind of resilience."[15] They found that environmental factors, such as the sorts of messages a person receives and believes, impact the development of one mindset or the other. Messages like "Find your passion" should be replaced with "Develop your passion," which encourages a growth mindset and deeper resilience.

This was a critical navigation aid for me to understand, to hear more clearly what was happening in my life. My seeming discomfort with how I do or don't participate in the relief of poverty and suffering around the world was like the small boat in the dark, discovering visibility reduced by the fog. It was a warning sign, not direction. My discomfort and restlessness could be better described as new awareness and new

---

15   Paul A. O'Keefe, Carol Dweck, and Greg Walton. "Having a Growth Mindset Makes It Easier to Develop New Interests." *Harvard Business Review*, September 11, 2018.

interest. How would we as a family respond—with a fixed mindset of interest or with a growth mindset of interest?

These new insights from Dr. O'Keefe allowed me to hear and understand more clearly about possibly charting a new course. It also helped me understand that I desired to go from "no action" to a state of "taking action" to address hunger and poverty in the world within my abilities. Finding my own voice would be the next step.

BELIEVING

In November 2016, I heard a thirty-year-old pastor from Tennessee was planting a new church in Georgetown called Veritas City Church. My wife and I prayed about it and agreed to join the new work, and that made all the difference.

I met several new people and discovered their many passions. Ms. Beatrice Smith, an amazingly godly woman, taught me to consider deeper prayers to our Creator. She also opened my eyes to needs in Georgetown I had never seen in the thirteen years of living in the area. We had our own homeless community, people in need, pain, and suffering that was being addressed by few. I also met a young seminary student from Georgia, Jordan Thigpen, whose own transformative story impacted me as I worked to walk the journey toward newfound purpose.

As a youth, Jordan's life goal was to smoke weed and get high every day for the rest of his life. But he grew, discovered new things, found faith in Jesus Christ, and it changed his life forever. When I interviewed him about this time in his life, he said, "I began to take leadership in my faith by serving at camps for school kids through the Fellowship of Christian Athletes, and I had no aspiration other than to just share what God had done in my life."[16] His season at camp became a period of all stop. He found navigation aids that eventually put him on the path to seminary, to meeting his lovely wife Macey, to starting a family and helping plant a church in Georgetown, and ultimately to being ordained as a pastor and answering a call to serve a church in Georgia, bringing his talents and faith to a people in need.

His story is inspirational to me. Because he is from Georgia and I am from Texas, we understood the subtleties of life that exist in some places, even in the 21st century. We shared our experiences of prejudice and racial hatred. In his story, I saw a man who found a mindset of interest, and though it was hard to have conversations with family and former friends, he pressed on toward his new faith and the chosen course of life to make disciples who live on mission.

Eventually, I was inspired to serve on the mission field and work in Washington DC, to bring the good news to the lost and broken-hearted. Getting to know Jordan, I found reconciliation for a wounded heart over things I'd experienced in Georgia. It was a beautiful step on my journey, to add forgiveness to my path. For Jordan, the decision to take leadership and ownership of the work at camp put him emotionally in a place where he could receive new opportunities. For me, the willingness to step into supporting a new church in

---

16 Jordan Thigpen, interview by author, July 26, 2018.

Georgetown put me in a place to receive grace and mercy and to love people.

NOT GIVING UP, BUT REMAINING FLEXIBLE TO THRIVE

So I discovered that I could have a growth mindset, develop a new interest and build up resilience. I discovered new opportunities for reconciliation and observed someone who inspirationally changed everything to follow Jesus. Now, confronted with new information, I discovered that my quest to help with hunger and poverty didn't necessarily need to be somewhere across the sea in Uganda or Malaysia. I could do something right now in Washington DC, right now. More importantly, I discovered that my choices were not constrained. Maybe I could leave full-time work, but maybe I didn't need to in order to serve. There may be options if I am willing to see them. In fact, maybe the opportunity was always right there, but I was not ready to see and serve.

In 2014, Ms. Shannon Kaiser, a best-selling author, speaker, and entrepreneur,

names three action steps that should be shared to finding purpose and passion:[17]

1. **Get More Action**
   You can't think your way into finding your life purpose; you have to do your way into it. Take a mental note from Nike and Just Do It. The more we act, the clearer we get

---

[17] Shannon Kaiser. "3 Unexpected Ways to Find Your Life Purpose." HuffPost. September 25, 2017.

on things. So instead of overthinking it—Will this work out? Should I try that? What if I don't like it? What if I don't make money at it? Start taking steps toward your goals and start trying new things. This will help you get out of your own way. I struggled for years trying to find out what my purpose was. This cycle only created a deeper lack of clarity. It wasn't until I started doing that things changed for me. I began writing and sent a story to *Chicken Soup for the Soul*. The second I received the letter of acceptance was unlike any ever before, love flooded into my heart and I knew this was what I had to do with my life. You see though, I had to start writing to learn that my biggest passion was indeed writing. That only came with consistent action.

The experience is the reward; clarity comes through the process of exploring. Action is where you get results.

2. **Drop From Your Head to Your Heart**
   Your heart is your best tool to access your true purpose and passion. Ask yourself what you love? Start taking steps to do what you love. When you are inspired and connected to your happy self, inspiration floods your heart and soul. When you lead from your heart, you are naturally more joyful and motivated to explore. By doing what you love, you will be inspired and gain insights into what brings you the most joy.

3. **Break Up with The "ONE"**
   Many of us struggle because we try to find that ONE thing we are meant to do; but trying to find only one thing is the reason why we feel like something is missing.

The notion we have only one thing we are meant for limits us in fulfilling our greatness. Take me, for example; I have seven different job titles. I'm a life coach, travel writer, author, speaker, teacher, mentor, designer, and each thing I do brings me joy, but none of these are my purpose, they are my passions. So start getting in touch with your passions! When you lead a passionate life, you are living your life on purpose.

Let go of thinking you have only one purpose and embrace the idea that our purpose in life is to love life fully by putting ourselves into our life! This means we jump in and try new things; we stop resisting the unknown and we fully engage in what is happening right here, where we are. To lead a purposeful life, follow your passions. When we live a passion-filled life, we are living on purpose, and that is the purpose of life.

Shannon Kaiser's last step is the key—are you willing to be willing? As Admiral Hewitt said, "It is not the destination but the journey that counts." Do you have what it takes to let go of old thoughts and the old ways of being? Let go, as Shannon Kaiser recommends, of the anchor holding you back. Open yourself to new opportunities, to receive new insight, to a place where you can thrive.

Let it go, and jump in.

REFLECTION AND DISCUSSION QUESTIONS
1. Have you felt lost? Felt like you are wandering and adrift? Are you willing to come to all stop!

2. Do you have a fixed mindset or a growth mindset? Are you letting fear blow you around like waves across the sea?
3. Have you felt something calling to you? Are you willing to be willing? What if this means a radical change in lifestyle, place of residence, or station? What really motivates your heart?
4. Do you know what you believe? How are you sharing that belief, even if it's with just your mentor?
5. Do you know Jesus Christ?

CHAPTER 10

AGE IS ONLY A NUMBER

Whether you think you can, or you think you can't, you're right.
—HENRY FORD

At fifty-four years old, I have a different view of life than I did at eighteen. While a senior at Abilene Cooper High School in Abilene, Texas, I wrote *If life were but one letter less, it would be a lie*, and I believed I was being profound. Now I see I was precocious.

I was trying to make a statement.

How can expression be a revelation of oppression?

Just after a rain, when we look closely, the colors in the forest are a little more vibrant.

PRESSURE AND RELIEF
What do you think of when they say that time heals all wounds?

As a teenager, I thought the phrase meant for someone to "just get over it."

As a teenager in the 1970s, I believed some things worked against me, like being an African American in the heart of the Texas Bible Belt. I wanted to be just a plain old regular kid, but I had a strike against me. I thought my choices were either go with the flow or get run over. I chose to go with the flow.

In contrast, Mrs. Genevieve Smith was born in 1934 near Paris, France, where her father served as a government official. She was raised in a free France. Then she had to live through the horrors of war and the occupation by the Nazi Germans.

When the occupation began, her family relocated to the beautiful Bordeaux region of southern France. They lived in a small sea-faring town at the mouth of Arcachon Bay, called Arcachon, which sits across the bay from the Peninsula of St. Jean Cap Ferrat, where the lighthouse stands.

For young Genevieve, the reality of growing up in an occupied country was not easy, but she was taught one lesson by her mother about the Nazi Germans—never accept chocolate from the Germans because it was poisoned.

While (probably) not literally true, it gave an impressionable young girl the warning to steer clear, and the warning has had a lifelong, lasting impact on her association of Germans and chocolate with poison.

In my case and in Genevieve's case, societal hurt surrounded us. Genevieve developed a view of the pressure in the context of bitter poison. I developed a view of the pressure in the context of going with the flow.

Experiencing pressure and finding relief was different for each of us.

BOLD ADVENTURE
Different only means different. Different does not connote value or infer comparison.

The two stories in the previous section of societal pressure showed how those pressures resulted in differing views.

Genevieve's adventures began to take shape in post-war France. As a young woman, she had aspired to public service, hoping to receive excellent training in the Army. Full of excitement, she was ready to begin her journey, but one afternoon she fell onto train tracks and her right foot was amputated by a train.

During her hospitalizations and the worst of her anguish and despair, she found solace in the writings of French writer Comte de Lautréamont. His writing spoke to her innermost soul and captured the depths of her anguish brilliantly. His poetic novel *Les Chants de Maldoror*, whose central figure, Maldoror, renounced conventional morality.

The wild, wandering pages of this French poetic novel gave Genevieve a needed empathetic soul in Maldoror. In the

"Songs" of Maldoror, she found order, a way to return to the world of the living and survive and thrive.

Although it took more than sixty years to have the opportunity, at the age of eighty-four, after surviving the death of her husband, Genevieve resolved to travel to Montevideo, Uruguay, to see the childhood home and birthplace of Lautréamont. For Genevieve, this trip, a lifetime in the making, was a passionate satisfaction of close kinship.

Technically, I have thirty years to reach eighty-four, then maybe I could stir up my passions to travel to Israel. That is what this book is about, and this chapter specifically—living passionately at any age.

It's bold and young at heart to travel from Georgetown to Uruguay at age eighty-four to see the birthplace of the writer whose work, by the time Genevieve had discovered it, was a century old.

To believe in something—this is the bold adventure.

NO BARRIERS
Belief makes us alive.

I learned from my friend Genevieve to accept no barriers to what inspires you. Regardless of life's pressures, a way out is always present, and a new beginning is possible.

An oft-quoted Chinese proverb aptly says, "Fall down seven times; rise eight." It is possible. So, get up.

When I was nineteen, I thought thirty-two was ancient and sixty meant someone was almost dead.

Now at fifty-four, I think the forties are the teenage years and thirties and under are still so young. I see vibrant people in their eighties. I know I can be just as marvelously curious in my eighties and nineties as I was as a teenager. So many things in the world have yet to be discovered.

The key to making those discoveries is not allowing the false idea of barriers to creep in. It doesn't matter how you were born or how others identify you. How do you see opportunities in the world?

Dream big. Love bold. Be alive!

REFLECTION AND DISCUSSION QUESTIONS
1. Is it okay to struggle with believing you are too old or too young?
2. Is it okay to be afraid of past hurts or not know how to stand against the pressures of your past?
3. Is it okay to take risks because you feel inspired or to not know what you want to do when you grow up?

CHAPTER 11

FEAR AND LOYALTY

So, first of all, let me assert my firm belief that the only thing we have to fear, is fear itself.
—FRANKLIN DELANO ROOSEVELT[18]

This quote from President Roosevelt's inaugural address was masterful. It can stand on its own, with no context, but absolutely resonate with anyone. As I consider these words, I am instantly drawn to the principal assumption. We are a team.

We are in all kinds of teams. Family teams. Sibling teams—biological or chosen through foster or adoption. Neighborhood teams. Town or state teams. Office project teams, like the coffee crew—going for coffee three days a week. We are identifiable as a group. We are a team.

Yet not all of us have had good experiences. Some of us have felt the sting of being picked last for a team—feeling

---

18 The Joint Congressional Committee on Inaugural Ceremonies." Franklin D. Roosevelt Inaugural Address. March 4, 1933. Accessed February 18, 2020.

undesired or unwanted. Some of us have felt the anguish of being rejected for a team we really wanted to be part of. Some of us have suffered silently, in the middle of the pack, as unfair actions were taken against others. But we kept quiet because we didn't want to be rejected and cast aside.

In September 2001, I was assigned to Marine Corps recruiting duty. I proudly served with a team of men and women, headquartered in Frederick, Maryland. At the time, I had only been with the team for fifteen months, just long enough to get a feel for the team and the work. I loved the mission.

I believed then, and still believe now, that it is noble to be of service to others, to be willing to serve in sacrifice to a cause—protecting our nation. I wanted to share that belief with young people, to give others the opportunity to see what I see, a chance to join something larger than themselves, and to be a part of the world's finest fighting force.

At that point in my career, I had already served the nation deployed with peacekeeping teams during the unrest in Monrovia, Liberia, during Desert Storm aboard the *USS Guadalcanal*, and during withdrawal operations in Mogadishu, Somalia. So, I had already learned fear is the worst of emotions. It can help drive heroic actions that cause victory in battle, but it can divide teams and usher in remarkable defeats.

A team must learn to manage fear, knowing that it can help and that it can also destroy.

TERRITORY AND THE CHALLENGE

In 1999, I worked for a Marine Corps Officer named Angela Salinas. She was the Director of Strategic Plans for the 3rd Marine Expeditionary Force headquartered in Okinawa, Japan. She was an exceptionally skilled leader and operations expert. I was inspired by her stories of being the Commanding Officer of a Marine Recruiting Station. Some days after work, she would talk to us about her career and impart lessons she had learned. It was an effective way to cultivate leadership within our group and build teamwork through transparency. Her talks helped create opportunities for us to learn from triumphs and mistakes and draw parallels in our own career experiences. Her experiences on recruiting duty inspired me to think differently—find quality candidates, even at the expense of short-term mission goals and set the bar high for the team.

Inspired by Colonel Salinas' stories, I tried to inspire the team to reach for the stars, hinting that college-bound high school students should have an opportunity to be part of the world's finest force. As a college student at the United States Air Force Academy, not all my friends graduated with me. Those who left school had their own unique story, but I had time to talk with them about their futures before they left school.

As I attempted to inspire the Marine recruiters to buy into my ideas, I had an occasion to conduct a ride-along with a recruiter who struggled with the idea. He had scheduled our visit to take me to a high school in Fauquier County, Virginia that he found impenetrable. The high school guidance counselors had forbidden military recruiter visits. As we walked in the door to visit the Head of the Guidance Counseling Department, I noticed a flyer about the Air Force Academy. Just after we shook hands, I shared with her that I was a graduate of the Air Force Academy and told her it was very exciting to see that she was giving her students information about the academy, giving them an opportunity to compete for appointments. I also said something about appreciating my own high school counselors helping me navigate the college process. Then I asked point-blank why she and the school didn't like military recruiters.

"What do you mean? We have the Army recruiter here all the time," she responded. The rest of the visit was very pleasant, or at least it was pleasant to me. However, the entire visit was eye-opening for the Marine recruiter showing me the ropes. He'd created a mental barrier, and the US Army Recruiter was taking advantage all day long.

We were not there to "get people," rather, we were there to share information. The Marine Corps offers great opportunities and adventure in the idea of "to protect what you love, stand and be counted." I love the United States and was willing to be counted.

I saw recruiting as an honor to serve the greater good. It was inspiring.

ONE STRANGE DAY
But then, in September 2001, just before September 11, during the middle of a morning meeting, an argument erupted between two of my most senior leaders. I was not

in the meeting, but because of the small size of our headquarters, I heard the loud escalation of voices and shuffling of furniture.

For this story, the specifics of the argument are not important but rather the root cause—fear. One person made a disrespectful comment, and the other person believed their work had been ridiculed. The trading of insults caused each to fear the loss of each one's "place" or "status."

Interestingly, both men were new to their positions and had not gelled with my leadership style. I had cultivated unity across the team, but they had not yet embraced how I was working with the team to advance everyone's goals, dreams, and career aspirations.

Both were incredibly talented and demonstrated exceptional skill. They are remarkable men, and I am still very proud to have served with them! However, at the time, because they were new and unsure of me, they misunderstood when I sent them home to cool off. I intended to individually have breakfast with each and settle the issue.

My most important mistake was allowing twelve hours to pass before handling it. I should have taken them to lunch together and hammered it to resolution. At the time, I thought I could divide and conquer their fears by giving them a little breathing room. I didn't realize that a battle would continue to be waged over the early evening hours. Not with me and not with each other, but with proxies. These two were not loyal to me because they did not know I was loyal to them. The next morning over breakfast, they found out that I was loyal, but they shared with me that their lack of trust in me caused them to take actions they perceived as self-preservation.

That day was not the battle, the next day was the real battle, and I would be in a very bad position.

FEAR AND BAD BEHAVIOR

Fear and time do not mix well.

The cooler heads I had hoped would be achieved overnight were actually simmering pots of fear. They did not know I was devoted to them individually, so later that evening, phone calls were made and allegiances drawn. By the time the sun had set, outsiders became involved, making it bigger than it should have been, all without consulting me. Driven by fear, the phone calls led to uncontrollable escalation. My superiors took control, and by 9 a.m. the next morning, jobs were lost, and I was given a new team and sternly warned.

This story is about people and the importance of loyalty. I learned three key steps for being on a team—build identity, cultivate mindset, and drive health.

REFLECTION AND DISCUSSION QUESTIONS

1. Do you enjoy being on a team? Are you willing to consider that you are on one of multiple types of teams—have you considered your role?
2. Have you captured your own lessons learned from being on a team?

3. Are you willing to acknowledge your own mistakes with the team? The team moves forward only when everyone participates equally.
4. What and who inspires you? Does anyone on your team know?
5. What do you think about fear? Always good — Always bad? Are you willing to consider the answer might be more of a shade of gray?

CHAPTER 12

SEE IT IN YOUR MIND AND CREATE

Innovation is truly a confusing buzzword which many people love to hate.

—NICK SKILLICORN[19]

When you feel inspired, does your mind drift?

I often feel a crazy sense of joy—and despair. This is rooted in an overpowering love for the accomplishment and a deep sorrow that I could spectate, not participate.

In high school, I played alto saxophone. I was not great but not bad. When I was a freshman, living in Anchorage, Alaska, an incredible senior scoffed at a young kid like me in the symphonic band. But I challenged him to the first chair, and

---

19 Roberto Battaglia, et al. "What Is Innovation? 15 Experts Share Their Innovation Definition." Idea to Value, November 4, 2016.

I won. The next week, he put me back in my place, but everyone respected me a little more.

He didn't just play in the symphonic band, he also played in the jazz band, and when I got to see him improvise, it was magical. His level of creative genius took a basic chord structure, and he could riff like water flowing from a glass. It was mesmerizing and beautiful.

At the same time, it was humbling. As desperately as I loved what I heard, I regretted my talent would never allow me to instantly join in and effortlessly be part of the beautiful music.

We have an infinite capacity to create and innovate. Some of you, like me, will see innovation in the abstract, not in a particular time or particular medium.

INNOVATION AND PERSPECTIVE

What is the relationship between technology, innovation, and the people who dream? Do we at the individual level decide not to create when we could have? Do we believe that the opinions of others hold our fate? Do we have ideas of innovative or technological change that are at the mercy of our peers or society at large? How many genius ideas are in remote villages in the Amazon Forest among a people who do not know of the modern world? Do you need to have a PhD in technology to have a brilliant idea?

CREATION INNOVATION
What seed sparks innovation?

In the abstract, many different ingredients result in a blend that makes an amazing creative result. For some, it may be seeing things in a new way. For others, it may be the long fermenting of an idea combined with new input, like yeast, which causes the innovation to rise. It might even be a location, where ideas finally drop into place.

I witnessed another example of genius that left me utterly in awe.

In 2011, my oldest child actually produced a working air-powered hoverboard. I had never seen that kind of mental genius. The project was called the French Diaspora. When the topic was first briefed to the teacher, Ms. Cameron, she did not have high hopes for the idea.

"I am not familiar with that word," said Ms. Cameron when informed of the project's idea.

The concept was to visually represent the "diaspora," the movement of indigenous people, on a creative representation of a globe of suspended lights. First was the idea that lights would be suspended and, in their illumination, would create a free-floating globe. Then the diaspora would be represented by flickering lights representative of larger or smaller populations.

Recounting it in words does not do justice to the idea, but just retelling it here, I am fascinated by the concept. Who thinks to create a suspended globe, with lights in specific locales flickering to denote larger and smaller populations representing the French diaspora?

I will never forget the night when the drills and saws came out and the project started taking shape. For over an hour, I watched holes being drilled in meticulous circles and labels being added to each hole.

Then there was a meticulous counting of suspension wire. So many at length one. So many at length two. So many at length three, and so on. At the end of each was prepared a suspended light bulb. A series of resistors and capacitors made the lights flash, but then each combination had a specific assignment and connection.

In the end, I saw it, the "globe of lights." I looked at it in silence, wondering how a mind can see that in a concept, a drawing, an idea, and then make it a reality. It was the second time I was really in awe. I reveled in the moment. I could never begin to create like this, but even more, I could not even dream like this.

Creation innovation. In the mind, the idea was born and with the hands, it was made into reality. This is breathtaking and life-giving all at the same time.

It gives me hope.

NEW THINKING AND NEW LIFE

I find hope in connecting my belief in the infinite to the concrete displays of creativity, such as hearing a genius create notes on a saxophone or watching genius envision a masterful representation and then using the hands to bring it to reality.

These small examples affirm anything is possible.

If it can be done, then each of us might be the one to do it. Each one has value, and who knows who is the next Pablo Picasso or Alice Walker? How do we know we are not seeing the work of the next Zheng Banqiao or reading the words of the next Fyodor Dostoevsky?

Thinking differently about the presence of the infinite in each of us means thinking differently about life and how we see it.

I have skills, talents, and abilities. One of those is to straighten up stray ends. I see trash on the ground, and I want to pick it up. In disorder, I see order and move to make it so. Is this just a quirk, or is it my unique means to create?

What does it mean if six billion people living on the planet each have something unique to share, to give, and to contribute? No one is insignificant.

Each person is unique and contributory.

HOW DO YOU MEASURE CONTRIBUTIONS AND CREATIONS?

Is it okay to find in the largest of things, beauty? Is it okay to see the immeasurable is the smallest of things, dedication? Is it okay to be amazed? Is it okay to not be in awe of something, wanting?

CHAPTER 13

PASSION'S REAL STORY

Life imitates Art far more than Art imitates Life.
— OSCAR WILDE[20]

The quote from Oscar Wilde's essay is one of many in the discussion of lying being an art and nature having flaws. A deeper look at the character's words expresses truth, even in the 21st century. People are often influenced by what they see, hear, and feel while watching fiction. Advertisers count on that as they sell millions of dollars of expertise to help sell products. What about "My music my way" or "You're in good hands" or "Just do it." These and others express concepts intended as a call to action. I see the call to action as potentially the highest form of life imitating art.

Passion is important in the pursuit of anything, and we should seriously consider the words of Oscar Wilde. Know

---

20 Oscar Wilde. The Decay of Lying: a Dialogue. London: K. Paul, Trench, 1889.

what you believe and feel. Understand what drives you and then act. Isn't that the beginning of passion's real story?

PASSION MISUNDERSTOOD

From 2011 to 2014, Dr. Paul O'Keefe held the Ruth L. Kirschstein National Research Service Award while a post-doctoral fellow at Stanford University. Against the beautiful backdrop of palm trees intermittently scattered amidst the lovely Spanish-influenced architecture of the campus, Dr. O'Keefe said, "The President of Stanford gave a commencement speech saying you have to go out there and find what you love, find your passion."

As a researcher, he determined to look at this more closely, to balance the idea expressed in the speech against research observations. Their research was published in 2018 titled "Implicit Theories of Interest: Finding Your Passion or Developing It."[21] As an example, Dr. O'Keefe and his colleagues observed a college graduate, exploring options to find her passions. She accepted a position in a biology lab but wasn't blown away by it. She moved to a second lab but wasn't blown away by it either. She then moved to a third and better lab and signed up to take graduate-level courses. On paper, she appeared to be doing all the right things, exploring her career path, but when viewed in terms of expectations, the research uncovered a different result. It was the difference in having a growth mindset or a fixed mindset. In her case, with a fixed mindset, you believe that interests are inherent within

---

21 Paul A. O'Keefe, Carol S. Dweck, and Gregory M. Walton. "Implicit Theories of Interest: Finding Your Passion or Developing It?" *Psychological Science* 29, no. 10 (October 2018): 1653–64. doi:10.1177/0956797618780643.

you, then if you encounter your interest or passion, it should awaken that interest. From that fixed mindset, your interest should just boil over. According to Dr. O'Keefe, "When she didn't encounter that overwhelming amazement of 'finding it,' she interpreted it as meaning 'there is nothing for me here.'"

Do the words of the President of Stanford represent art? According to Oscar Wilde, you could validly say yes. The words at this commencement, as well as at thousands of others, enticed graduating students with a picture-perfect image for them to set their expectations. "Go out there and find your passion." According to Dr. O'Keefe, when those words land on the ears of a new graduate with a growth mindset, they will naturally expect obstacles as part of their story. But for those with a fixed mindset, the words give them something to imitate. When they aren't blown away by an experience, they just move on—over and over again.

The misunderstanding of the role of passion is not isolated to just college graduates. Startup technology entrepreneurs and seasoned career professionals also want to follow passions. If not well armed with an understanding of growth mindset or fixed mindset, passions could be foiled, resulting in a season of drifting from one thing to the next—the tragic ending being a slow aging of a charred ember of a dulled flame.

THE FUEL THAT MOTIVATES

Have you ever been gripped by an idea? There you are, minding your own business, and then BAM! An all-consuming idea hits you.

Discovering passion and purpose led me on a journey to find experts and learn from their experiences, including Renu Ahluwalia, a technologist in Arlington, Virginia.

Meeting Renu Ahluwalia was like touching lightning, which carries up to 100 million volts of electricity. It is an unpredictable raw power that changes everything. She shared about her technology experiences and her devotion to teaching others to embrace technology. In an interview with her, she described the emergence of an idea at six years old. Renu Ahluwalia said, "I heard a story about children in need at school one day, so I went home, told my parents the problem, and told them what their part was in helping her achieve the goal of impacting those children."

This was clearly not an example of life imitating art, but life being the creator itself. Clearly a woman with a growth mindset, Renu did not wait, did not ask—she simply took hold of the issue, gave direction, and made the answer come to life. Moments like this are defining and set the course for a lifetime by their power. They bring a passion that takes hold of your soul from the inside out, and it transforms you.

I learned that age is not the determiner of either passion, leadership, or clarity of direction. At six years old, Renu set a course for a lifetime. This defining moment gave her the inner passion to achieve new heights, regardless of circumstance.

But others, like the author, entrepreneur, and pioneer Scott Dinsmore, find defining moments over time. In 2012, Scott Dinsmore shared his findings and passion in a San Francisco

TEDx where he educated audiences about finding work you love. He wore a purple shirt that day and smiled with disarming confidence that captivated his audience. I know because it captivated me. Purple is arguably the color worn by nobility and royalty, and with 70 percent of communication conveyed non-verbally, the choice conveyed the importance of his message.

One day, Scott said to a friend, "Let's work out at the greatest gym in the world." They spent the day using kettle weights, doing burpees, and running along trails all within full view of the Golden Gate Bridge. That day, Scott Dinsmore gave his friend the gift of seeing the world around you differently. This is another example of life not imitating art, but life giving life.

I believe we close our eyes to what is around us for many reasons—fear, anticipation, or loneliness to name a few. But just because our eyes are closed, the story is not complete. And just because our eyes are open, it does not mean that we fully see.

Scott Dinsmore found passion and a purpose to enjoy and fully live life right where he was. Love the life you live.

In 2015, Scott finished his time on earth. Up to the moment he passed, while climbing the summit of Mount Kilimanjaro, he lived the example he taught in his lesson. Do not be afraid.

Be alive! Live, love, give!

Just go!

DON'T WAIT

In my journey attempting to understand passion and motivations, these lessons from Dr. Paul O'Keefe, Renu Ahluwalia, and Scott Dinsmore make me want to go for a ride until the rims fall off!

I love the idea that the world's greatest gym may be right in the backyard. Whether you are in your New Jersey townhome, the crowded streets of Milan, Italy, a gently sloping roadway in Reykjavik, Iceland, or a winding roadway on the outskirts of Kabul, Afghanistan—the world is beautiful. Love and live where you are today!

I have a growing passion and clarity for the story of the rest of my life. I want to step foot onto the Continent of Antarctica! I want to drink lemonade in Cape Town, South Africa! I want to travel the entire length of Chile and have brunch in Punta Arenas! I want to feel rainwater on my face in the Amazon forest! I want to ride in a balloon over the Serengeti, peacefully observing the wildlife in the beautiful morning sunlight! I want to visit the trailhead of the summit trek to Mt. Everest, to pause and celebrate the life of the many lost Sherpas—giving a measure of respectful value to those who gave their lives in sacrifice of serving others by guiding them on the climb attempting to fulfill their dream achievement.

But all these ideas of traveling the world and living life to the fullest, to me they are vanity. Is it truly a passionate desire to 'live life' or is it an expression of my affluence? Would I not be just spending money I have saved on myself, treating myself to vainglorious adventures that really and truly only benefit me? Would I post any of these images on Facebook? Is that sharing life with others or trying to be part of the 'in-crowd,' showing that I too can live a cool life? Is this really what I want? No, it is not.

My growing passion is to help with homelessness and hunger.

This is the passion stirring within my heart. I know that I may not be capable of solving the problem, but like the little boy throwing starfish into the ocean, I can help one.

REFLECTION AND DISCUSSION QUESTIONS
1. Do you ever feel like you missed the boat? Are you willing to think with a growth mindset that such obstacles are okay, and you should keep going?
2. Do you know the moment when an idea grabbed you? Are you nurturing that idea, or have you jumped into the pool?
3. Do you love the life you live? Have you stopped to open your eyes to see the truly beautiful all around you, right where you are today? Are you willing to try?
4. Even if you can't solve world hunger, isn't it worth it to feed one or two or three while you try?
5. Which mindset do you have? Growth mindset or Fixed mindset?

SECTION III:

PROGRESS

CHAPTER 14

CONSIDER – THEN DREAM

Technology is nothing. What's important is that you have a faith in people, that they're basically good and smart, and if you give them tools, they'll do wonderful things with them.
—STEVE JOBS[22]

It starts with a dream, and the dream has its roots in a problem that needs to be addressed. Just because it cannot be done today, does not mean that it cannot be done.

Years ago, I was given a problem to update a list of people's names and addresses. The concern was the amount of time it took considering the constantly changing names, the difficulty in reorganizing names in precedence order, and then distributing a newly printed list. Initially, the effort was sadly

---

22 Jeff Goodell. "Steve Jobs in 1994: The Rolling Stone Interview." *Rolling Stone*, June 25, 2018.

tedious, which explained why it was only done once per year, but there had to be a better way. That's how I created a database and graphical user interface with a macro to provide the standardized output.

I wish this was a great story, but it was a lesson learned the hard way. I went from spending two minutes telling someone to make a new list to spending fifty minutes showing someone how to make the database and macro work. Overall, the total time needed to perform the task was greatly reduced but not my personal time.

So was this progress? I argue yes. It was the progress of an early adopter.

It has been said widely that staying still is dying, moving forward is living.

SEE THE NEED FOR CHANGE
In 2016, Faith Florez was a high school student in Central California. She saw a problem that needed to be addressed—migrant workers in Central California labor in extreme temperatures picking delicate produce. Central California contains one of the most active growing areas in the United States and has an endless need for farm workers. But to Faith, the need for change was obvious—farm workers needed to receive alerts when they should drink water or take action to reduce risk. She said in an interview published by Veronica Acosta, "The application is ultimately

designed to prevent instances of heat stroke amongst agricultural workers."[23]

Faith is inspirational to me because she did not let circumstances keep her from trying to solve the problem. She did not let her lack of age, lack of connections, or lack of a fully developed business plan deter her. That type of determination has sparked technology change for the good of all humanity.

She also inspires me to go for it. As a co-founder of Zoomiee, a tech startup in Austin, Texas, I have felt intimidated by obstacles—funding, operations challenges, and legal challenges to name just a few. When experience, customer-focused goals, and aspirations coalesce, the opportunities to pour my heart and soul into my work make sense. But new ventures, with long-term hopes potentially in jeopardy, with no runway left to recover, seem risky. But the inspirational message of Faith's example is *give your all to help people, no matter the cost.* That is bold dreaming and a call to review conviction about the nature of a problem.

If I really understood the problem, wouldn't I give my all to help? That's the dilemma of the older entrepreneur—little margin for error because time will not slow down. What is the fallback plan? However, on the other hand, no one is guaranteed another day, so take a chance!

---

23 Yara Simón. "This Teen Invented Calor, An App That Aims to Keep Farmworkers Safe in Hot Weather." Remezcla, April 11, 2018.

DREAMING OF CHANGE

With respect to taking a chance, however, I am an example of failure.

In college, I learned differential equations, physics, aerospace engineering, and organic chemistry. Despite what could have been a lifelong learning in the sciences, I never went further or used those lessons learned in my working career. I'm more of an art and music lover. But underneath it all still stirs a scientific wannabe.

For over fifteen years, I strongly felt our modern view of gravity was wrong. We misapplied what Einstein theorized. I have been encouraged by the ideas of symmetry and quantum gravity discussed in Tokyo at the Kavli Institute for the Physics and Mathematics of the Universe—fundamentally, that gravity is an energy source. We look at it wrong, not recognizing it is the universally available clean energy source. I wanted to uncover the truth of this and give it away to all of humanity. I want to see every human on the planet have access to light, heat, computational, and communications resources at negligible cost. Transportability in this new era will make every square inch of the globe accessible and food availability universal.

Anti-gravity and gravity as power resources will allow travel in and around our solar system. I am not certain of the chemistry of making breathable air on Jupiter but having the power resources to create a habitat will be achievable.

Without science or math to prove these things, they seem like science fiction. But a dream starts somewhere, and mine starts here. It is only a spark, now freely given to everyone to ridicule, investigate, or achieve a real scientific discovery.

None of these ideas have seen the light of day until now. My first step was opening myself to criticism. My next step is to build up the resolve to study and discover math and science to prove it.

I dream bigger—thanks to Faith Florez.

REFLECTION AND DISCUSSION QUESTIONS
1. Who inspires you? Are they older? Are they younger?
2. Do you have a dream?
3. What are you willing to give away?
4. Can you give someone else the credit and accept that it may come to life by someone else's effort?
5. What if all heating, cooling, light, computer power, and memory storage were gravity-powered and free?

CHAPTER 15

INNOVATION AND THE PASSIONATE

―

Douglas Engelbart kicks off the personal computer revolution, at Brook's Hall, with a product demonstration that inspired a generation of technologists.

—DYLAN TWENEY[24]

When you look at a brick, what do you see? The oven-tested clay? A three-dimensional rectangle? The beginning of a foundation?

When I look at a brick, I see the kinetic potential of gravity pulling it to the ground. How you see an object will determine what you draw as its potential to become part of something bigger.

---

24 Dylan Tweney. "Dec. 9, 1968: The Mother of All Demos." Wired. Conde Nast, September 11, 2018.

How can we explore the possibilities to think and challenge the status quo? How do we find the wonder in wonderful?!

To see possibilities, you must start by believing the impossible is possible.

INNOVATION AND PASSION

Innovation and passion are the same end to a quest to make mankind better, and it starts with believing the impossible is possible.

Many explore the world with the view that all there is, is all there is. When the universe came into existence with a bang, all that would ever exist was created. All the atoms needed to create anything came into being at once.

This finiteness shapes how we see every new idea or concept. If all there is, is all there is, then nothing new truly happens—it is only a repackaging of what was before. More importantly, if you have an idea for something new, you must take away from something else to allow the new idea you have to come into being.

The idea of finiteness distracts from an open review of innovation.

Consider for a moment the amazing power of a black hole. An astronomical wonder, where even light cannot escape as gravity reduces a great mass to an infinitesimal singularity. Is this the hypothesized destiny of the universe, over trillions of millennia, the universe will crash together and BANG! New reality begins?

Contrast this with the idea of an infinite creator—truly infinite, then omnipotent, omniscient, omnipresent, and eternal. From the viewpoint of an infinite creator, the idea of creating something from nothing is possible—true innovation IS POSSIBLE. A creator can at all times make something from literally nothing.

So, the finite point of view and the infinite point of view impact innovation, creativity, and imagination. However, these two views balance innovation and passion. It is not a case of 'either-or' but rather 'both-and.'

This is where the power of innovation grows. In healthy tension between two opposing views.

But 'both-and' is possible. In the world of startups and entrepreneurs, failure in a finite view has resulted in remarkably successful pivots. One direction may prove wrong, but a pivot in another direction, with experience and lessons learned, may just be the teacher needed to catapult the entrepreneur to exponential success.

This is what happened when I started a real estate development firm in 2001. I had my eye on a property for development in Western Maryland. I had spoken with the landowner of 140 acres and had envisioned the value the developed property would bring to the community. I met with an investment banker and learned the process of getting a business loan for $1 million dollars and believed it was attainable. I incorporated, hired staff, started paying salaries and payroll taxes.

Within a year, I was out of business. I had learned a lot, but still, I failed.

I started a consulting business to share my insights around the country. A business that has also not prospered.

I started a business with a direct sales company.

I also became a real estate agent, selling residential property in the greater Washington DC area. I met amazing people, buying and selling homes, but I also experienced a loss of time with my own family.

I misjudged the need to have a more settled family perspective, and I didn't know my own priorities. Money losses you can always earn back, but time can never be regained.

In this endeavor, it took sixteen years to unceremoniously end.

Failure, failure, failure, failure. Many ideas generated, not one yielded the success intended. Did the businesses work or did I fail to work the businesses?

The lesson here is about learning to be open to a new idea.

Are you open to a new idea?

Innovation begins where opportunity is in view.

PROGRESS

From a finite view, my story may look like failure and lots of it. From an infinite view, it may look like iteration. Each new turn was a new lesson, onward and upward.

There is beauty in watching a process run. Like seeds being scattered by a farmer, iteration has the opportunity for tremendous growth. A seed has amazing potential to become something huge, alive, thriving, and providing for the needs of others.

So does iteration.

Progress to something new and wonderful may seem slow at first, with the growth being imperceptible. Digging it up removes the potential. A few failures could seem like the imperceptible growth of the seed, but viewed with the fullness of the experience, it was part of the chain of actions required to arrive at an amazing result.

Growth, like success, is achieved one step at a time.

Iteration is just one step at a time.

Progress is beautiful—one step at a time.

To succeed is to try. To try is to fail. And to fail is how we win.

HOW DO YOU MEASURE PROGRESS AND PASSION?
1. Is it okay to see things in the finite? Is it okay to instead see things in the infinite?
2. How do seeds of passion grow under the water of adversity and disappointment? Can we truly innovate from our comfort zone?

SECTION IV:

PEOPLE

CHAPTER 16

PRIORITY – 177 PEOPLE

Who you hang out with determines what you dream about and what you collide with. And the collisions and the dreams lead to your changes. And the changes are what you become. Change the outcome by changing your circle.
—SETH GODIN[25]

According to Seth Godin's quote, when you change your circles, your outcomes can change. That was the case for me in September 2018 when I interviewed Renu Ahluwalia. She spoke of having a willingness to surrender to the now and then to inspire others. "Accepting where it is, IS where it is," said Renu.

Inspiring others to trust you and go with you. I felt willing to trust her and to philosophically go along for the ride. That's leadership.

---

25 Kickstarter. "Tina Roth Eisenberg: The Best Way To Complain Is To Make Things." YouTube video.
Nov 16, 2016.

Ultimately, leadership is about the people.

I have found as co-founder of a startup that it is hard to make the time when your mind is divided. "Accepting where it is, IS where it is." That is hard when so many competing dreams and goals are at work in your brain. Above it all, however, I have a complete and unrelenting priority, a love for people.

People are always first.

MAKE TIME

In 2017, I was fortunate to be selected to participate in the Startup Leadership Program—DC, a world-class training program for founders, leaders, and innovators. The selection process looked at leadership, entrepreneurial, and innovation experience, the potential for success in the startup ecosystem, willingness to be an active member of the startup community, and cultural fit with core values. Along with other founders from non-profit social justice startups and several founders of various tech startups including gaming tech, medical tech, education tech, and social networking tech, the program provided the opportunity to interact with innovators and companies ranging from early-stage ideation to pre-revenue minimum viable product stage. All of us seeking to add value to the world.

One of the founders, Alyssa Vazquez, had one of the most compelling ideas of integrating anthropology, technology, and the faith community in a very real and personal way. At the core of her product, in pre-production at the time, was the foundational idea that "no one should do life alone." I was inspired by the enduring truth and wisdom of the product idea. Her start-up idea represents the pure intersection of people, purpose, and innovation. Her idea means people are intrinsically linked, and technology can facilitate that to reduce the separation we naturally build up in our difficult interactions.

Alyssa Vazquez, the founder of YouBelong, is a dreamer; she has the ability to dream in five dimensions. She can see not only the new innovation but also the resulting world that will be created—more connected and resilient. She used a lens of compassion to see beyond today to a seamlessly connected tomorrow.

This is an example of leadership. Demonstrating a willingness to surrender to the now and then to inspire others.

LOVE THE PEOPLE
To surrender to the now, to have a clear sense of priorities, both these technologist leaders reinforced my fundamental beliefs and love for people.

The year was 1997. I was the Company Commander of a reinforced Marine Rifle Company. We were a task-organized company with a platoon of amphibious assault vehicles (AAV).

I was the senior Marine aboard the ship and the Commanding Officer of Troops aboard the *USS Harpers Ferry*.

One morning, while participating in a landing exercise off the coast of Australia, the storm winds blew, and the seas violently rocked the ship back and forth, presenting an added element of danger to this landing. But in addition, this landing was being observed by the Marine three-star general in command of Marine Forces Pacific. This landing was a big deal for my boss's boss, a chance to demonstrate his tactical acumen.

I had issued orders to the Marine landing forces on board, and we all made preparations; however, I was periodically informed of the storm's severity. As a team, we had made dozens of landings over a two-year period, so I had a feel for what was a problem and what was not. But THIS morning, I was given a specific warning by the Platoon Commander of the AAVs. "Sir, the sea state is at the edge of our safety limits," said 1st Lieutenant Howard Hall.

I, however, really wanted the landing to go well because the general was on the beach watching. I wanted it to succeed.

***

In the final hours before they launched from the ship, the men followed a standardized protocol:

- Finalize a review of the plans for the assault
- Issue final instructions
- Draw weapons, training ammunition, and perform pre-combat inspections
- Prepare AAVs for landing

- Conduct final safety inspections and dress rehearse ship-to-shore movements
- Brief the final water safety plan for AAVs as weapons systems and transport craft
- Load craft and prepare for the launch.

All the Marines spent the final three hours before launch getting ready. But I was focused on one thing—mission success.

At sea, the captain of the ship has final authority over everyone on board for safety. Even though the sea state was difficult, I trusted Captain Tangredi to determine safety parameters for the launching of craft. He also knew the significance of the exercise and who was observing. I was focused on the outcomes.

After loading the craft and getting set for launching, the ship made its final maneuvers to arrive at the launch point for AAVs. Everything was still given a green light; we would make the landing.

I climbed into the AAV and was last to load, confirming that the troops would make the assault. As I shut the hatch, First Lieutenant Hall said to me, "Sir, I recommend we not launch. The sea state is too dangerous." This was his second warning that morning.

This time, I was clear and succinct with him. "I understand. Prepare to launch AAVs."

Then he said, "For the record, I advised you that we not launch."

Sensing the finality and understanding his intent, I responded, "Noted, Lieutenant. On my authority proceed."

Then the launch doors of the bay were opened, and I could see for myself the sea swell. I knew it could be done.

Then the ship turned into the seas for launch. Everything changed.

Now I could see the actual height of the waves. In a flash, I considered my promise to bring home all 177 men. The captain of the ship signaled with a green light in the bay to launch AAVs. I was in the lead vehicle, and all the others would follow. In five seconds, I calculated in my head the nature of the real problem. In the high sea state, a significant probability existed that a craft with its troop doors opened would become waterlogged.

However, in 75 percent of our landings, one craft always had problems making it to the shore under their own power. Would the crewmen get out before the craft sank? Could this sea state cause men to lose their lives because I ordered the landing? What was the potential price, to impress the commanding general during a training exercise?

"Abort, abort, abort," I ordered into the headset while simultaneously opening the compartment door above my head as a secondary means of assuring the vehicle would stop its forward progress.

"We are not launching," I said into the internal headset to the Vehicle Team, quickly switching my communications headset over to the Landing Force Command frequency. "This is Texas Pete Six, get me Lone Wolf."

Over the two years we had worked together, I made a commitment to these men that they were the priority. Not my success or career. Here, in five seconds, it was put to the test.

That day, regardless of the cost to me, I decided that I loved people more.

REFLECTION AND DISCUSSION QUESTIONS
1. What are your priorities? Where do people stack on the list?
2. Are you willing to surrender to the now?
3. How do you view connectedness and resilience?
4. What would inspire you to put people first?

CHAPTER 17

FIRST TEARS, THEN A FRESH START

There is a lot to be done yet. But this is the right beginning. Listen.
—GEORGE ORWELL'S CHARACTER U PO KYIN[26]

Inspiration and fear live so closely together it can be hard to tell where fear ends and inspiration begins.

This is the story of a technologist. She is brilliant, vibrant, and alive. This is also the story of how my fears and successes have intersected with her story and provided new insights into my own life.

In 2015, I was selected, along with one hundred of my government peers, to attend a month-long in-residence course at the Federal Executive Institute (FEI) in Charlottesville,

---

26 George Orwell. *Burmese Days.* (Houghton Mifflin Harcourt, 1974).

Virginia. The course was Leadership in a Democratic Society and was designed to transform the way senior executives work together, learn together, and drive high-performing organizations to new levels of achievement.

Within the first forty-eight hours, I recognized most of the executives attending shared a common trait: we all were goal-oriented, high-achieving leaders, dedicated to the missions of our various organizations.

Within ninety-six hours, I discovered something else as the professors exposed us to more of the traits of senior executives and the highest level of leaders in government: I was not worthy of that high call. I was selected but unworthy.

It was a gripping revelation.

It was only the second time in my life I felt so emotionally overwhelmed. The previous time was in college during another leadership team building event. The instructor of that event was very upset with me as I lagged behind the others; he told me in no uncertain terms that I was a waste of humanity, I didn't deserve to breathe, and the best thing I could do for everybody was to quit, so I wouldn't be responsible for getting somebody killed.

I was overflowing with emotion at the time, but I steeled myself, clenched my teeth, and told myself that what he said may, in fact, be true, but I wasn't quitting. They could send me home, but I was never quitting.

I felt the same rush of emotion that afternoon at FEI. I was among an amazing group of executives, but I absolutely didn't belong there. I wasn't sure how to handle it.

I feel a little of the same here, tears on my keyboard as I write. I don't know how to write or to share with you the ideas in my mind, and I feel like a total failure.

There it is. The truth. But only half of the truth.

The other half that I cannot explain well is what is inside of me. You don't see it or hear it, but when you see me smiling at a random person on purpose, you know there's something. When you see me with earbuds in, moving to some music I'm listening to as though no one was around, you know something is different. When you see me randomly stop and smell a flower or spend three or four minutes with my smartphone out taking a picture of a flower from a few different angles, you know something is not quite the same.

To help you understand me better, I have taken the Myers-Briggs Type Indicator test, found at mbtionline.com. It indicated I am aligned with type INFP, which means I make decisions based on feelings.

I took the test at FEI and afterward, in the room full of executives, I learned only five of us in the room shared the same trait. We were told the "feeling" type decision-makers comprised less than 4 percent of all executives in the federal government.

It was a lightbulb revelation for me.

I thought, "No wonder!"

My whole working career had been frustrating. I felt I was always pushing against most everyone else. It felt like no one ever sees what I see or gets what I am driving at. Over my career, I found it necessary to develop one-on-one opportunities to use my impassioned pleas to explain my perspectives and persuade others to be motivated by my ideas.

I seek to be understood, as we all do.

DISCOVER SELF, DISCOVER FUTURE
The first time I heard Ron Hewitt say, "Discover self, discover future," I fiercely rejected it. He is an inspirational leader whom I greatly respected at the time, but in my mind, the conclusion was wrong.

I thought, *Look! We're trying to get someplace. The journey is fine, but we are trying to arrive at a destination.*

In his quote, I heard, "It doesn't matter where we are going, let's just go together." Though that is not what he said, I heard a specific conclusion—"go."

I felt the conclusion should be—"arrive."

I have always believed myself to be the tortoise. I must work longer and harder than all the rest. They are smarter than I—better equipped. I have to continuously work to reach the finish line, not necessarily to win but to arrive on time.

In the conversation above with Ron, where the journey was described as key, I again found myself between inspiration and fear. To me, the destination has always been crucial.

To know where you are going gives you the ability to plan your route, to assess your own capabilities, and establish estimates of your achievable speed. It also allows you to set up measures and milestones to allow you to check your progress along the way. This is how a tortoise views life. One measured event leading to another.

Six years later, I believe Ron Hewitt's comment is true, but I have had difficulty understanding how to put it into practice. I am still a tortoise, but now I understand that on the journey, we discover who we are and what we believe.

I am an INFP, and in 2018, I began trying to discover beauty in the other personality types.

So, I thought I'd start with someone more concrete and fact-oriented. You know, sciencey. I thought I should learn from a technologist.

Candace Faber is a brilliant and fiercely independent technologist. She was recruited while in college to join the U.S. Department of State as a Foreign Service Officer.

A respected thought leader, she edited the 2008 edition of the Georgetown Press publication, *Careers in International Affairs*. As a diplomat, she has spoken internationally and represented the State Department to a gathering of foreign diplomats. In 2010, she gave an example talk where she spoke in Poland educating diplomats on the benefits of technology helping to drive social change and advance the LGBTQI rights movement.

Here is an example of a fact-based, high-functioning thought leader helping educate others about the advent of technology concerning the rights of the individual. Technology drives beliefs.

However, not everyone in the department could see what she saw. She had a stage to influence foreign diplomats around the world, but our own US diplomats did not always come to conclusions similarly.

She told me a story of her time at the US Embassy in Kabul, Afghanistan where she reached the boiling point.

In Kabul, she wanted to do her job, going out to meet with local Afghan officials. Because of the nature of the environment with Taliban fighters still having significant influence, she had to request to leave the US Embassy compound to make the visit with Afghan officials. Her request was submitted, but it was determined the local environment was too volatile and dangerous. The dichotomy, however, was that the same risk calculation was not applied to native Afghan interpreters.

Candace said, "The Department of State, or at least my superior, was not ready to accept uncertainty and loss of control." [27]

---

27   Candace Faber, interview by author, July 25, 2018.

When her request to travel into town was denied for the safety of US diplomats, the task was then put in the form of an order given to a native Afghan interpreter.

It was a clear understanding of the value she saw in human life. Somehow, the rules for determining risk to human safety seemed to be applied differently. The native Afghan interpreters were ordered to go into these risky environments to attend meetings. On the surface, it seemed as though human life was regarded in one way for the US diplomats and another way for the native Afghan interpreters.

She called the dichotomy out. She told her superior that since the risk to human safety was too high, the native Afghan interpreters could not be ordered to such meetings. But the result was not good.

"I was labeled a troublemaker," she said.

Frustrated, she asked for a leave of absence and traveled to Cambodia.

SET YOU FREE
Then you will know the truth, and the truth will set you free.
—JESUS (JOHN 8:32 NIV)

In Candace's experiences in Afghanistan, I see a lesson about my views of scientific thinkers.

I was wrong to think that only one way of thinking means success. I misapplied my experience of having repeatedly failed to impress upon others my concerns. I had to repeatedly go over the same idea three or four times before someone else would get what I meant. It was the problem of me being in the 4 percent and others in the 96 percent.

I decided if only I weren't a feely thinker, then I could share ideas with ease.

Candace's experiences taught me that scientific thinkers who express their ideas do not automatically meet with success. Even scientific thinkers arrive at the same destination a feeling thinker would.

It gives me hope.

It should give you hope. You are free to think and be who you are. The destination you seek can be achieved following the wonderfully successful way of thinking you were born with—whatever that way of thinking might be.

The lesson continued as I followed Candace's story to Cambodia.

She was finally alone and free to think and explore her goals. Candace tells the story of picking up George Orwell's book *Burmese Days* and in reading it, she found a kindred spirit.

In following along with Orwell's main character, she found profound similarities to her story. She was a government worker, and the main character was a government worker.

She became steeled in her resolve. She resigned from the Foreign Service and started over. She went back to her beginning. She returned to her family in Utah and devoted time to tracing her heritage.

Candace said, "I interviewed family members, collected stories and their recollections."[28]

But the journey of reconnecting and emerging renewed with a sense of purpose was not simple. She was the serious accident that required a year-long recovery.

This was the real catalyst of change in how she saw herself.

THE FUTURE, AND FREEDOM

I invented nothing new. I simply assembled the discoveries of other men behind whom were centuries of work.

—HENRY FORD

Candace emerged from this year-long road to recovery knowing she was fundamentally a technologist, resolved to tackle social issues with technology, passion, and perseverance. She then moved to Seattle with no real plan but to hang out with tech people.

"The challenge for us is to take this incredible knowledge and passion and expertise that live in the social sector and

---

28 Ibid.

philanthropy and combine it with some of this fresh energy and insights from the tech community."[29]

The growth of the technology industry in Seattle brought in great minds and skilled code developers, data scientists, and programmers. But the flood of tech talent also changed the local economy and affordable housing options. The number of homeless grew as the wave of tech talent flooded in.

As the problem grew, Candace and others in the technology space began looking to use their competencies to apply them to the homeless situation. She got involved in the 'Hack to End Homelessness' effort and within a year was being asked to speak across the region.

She accepted a city government position with Seattle as the city's first Civic Technology Advocate, but again she detected discordant views. This time, in the tech community itself. She found a subtle preference for a tech solution rather than a fully informed understanding. Tech for the sake of tech, not addressing real problems at their root and core.

Candace found those creating technology to be arrogant.

"They were not really looking or understanding the needs or concerns of the marginalized," she said.

This painful lack of empathy struck home as a close friend, a brilliant technologist, suffered mental health issues, was

---

[29] Lisa. Stiffler. "Interview: Candace Faber, Seattle's First 'Civic Technology Advocate,' on Tech for Change, and How to Save Seattle." GeekWire, August 11, 2016.

arrested, and fell into the cycle of clinics and homeless shelters. None of the 'tech bros' even wanted to try to understand.

The lesson: One style of thinking and reasoning does not equate to smooth sailing. Where I felt emotionally overwhelmed at FEI, as though I was unworthy and undeserving, I was wrong. I arrived at the wrong conclusion and Candace's amazing story helped me see that—the 96 percent don't just automatically win. Where I had encapsulated the issue to be binary, I discovered there to be an amazing degree of nuance all around.

It is like being renewed. Given the opportunity to step up and try another at-bat.

HOW DO YOU MEASURE FREEDOM TO CHOOSE AND BE DIFFERENT?
1. Is it okay to not feel the same as others? Is it okay to feel ashamed of who you are? Filled with limitations? Filled with beauty and strength but not the real you?
2. What does it mean to feel alone in a crowded room? What does it mean to sleep in a bed with someone and feel empty and unknown?
3. Is it okay to hope for something new?

CHAPTER 18

TEARS UPON SEEING THE NEED

We think sometimes that poverty is only being hungry, naked, and homeless. The poverty of being unwanted, unloved, and uncared for is the greatest poverty.

—MOTHER TERESA[30]

I am moved to tears when I see someone in need. Don't get me wrong, I'm as callous as anyone. If I detect the slightest hint of insincerity, they don't get a second glance. But while visiting Texas in 2018, I saw my dad moved to tears, which moved me to tears.

My father had been diagnosed with dementia. So small tasks were big tasks because there were a thousand questions. For

---

30 Catholic Online. "Mother Teresa Quotes - Mother Teresa of Calcutta." Catholic Online. Accessed February 19, 2020. https://www.catholic.org/clife/teresa/quotes.php.

anyone who has not been there, seeing a parent's memories slip away is not fun.

We were running errands during an otherwise unremarkable sunny afternoon in Austin. We had been riding around for about twenty minutes with me at the wheel and my father quiet in the passenger's seat.

We were in a line of cars waiting to leave the parking lot and enter the roadway as we left Walmart, and I could tell something was bothering him. He started to fidget and then he started to mumble to himself and make small noises.

"Everything okay, Dad?" I asked.

He looked at me with tears running down his cheeks and said, "I don't like seeing women with children panhandling like that. I just don't. We should help her."

That was it. I lost it.

This is the most important question we face in our lives as we strive to live for what matters.

What makes you cry?

INNER STRENGTH
My dad reached into his pocket and pulled out a hundred-dollar bill as I rolled down the window on his side.

He handed it to her and said, "I'm sorry."

I was a wreck.

I had rarely seen my father cry when I was a boy. With my dad having lost some of his memory, I felt like I was seeing him at his core in this state. The real him, unvarnished by mental protections. On display was real emotion about what he saw. He saw someone in need, was moved to tears, and he acted.

Simple.

The encounter made me rethink what is important and why.

Every single human being has meaning and an infinite purpose. Life is a gift. All human life is connected. Each of us has something that matters.

What is that for you? Knowing what matters to you gives you inner strength and satisfaction.

For me, it is people. Knowing that causes me to ask more questions. If we are all connected, like parts of a body, how can we damage one another? Isn't there an intrinsic value we ascribe to each other? Despite our distinctness, we see the criticality of the whole. Each has a distinctive role, vital, critical, and necessary to the entire whole.

What does it mean that others do not share my beliefs? But it is not necessary to share my views because truth will be uncovered in eternity. Until then, I focus on what matters to me, as you should decide what matters to you and focus there.

Gabor Mate, a physician who specializes in development and childhood trauma, tells an amazing story about knowing one's self.

> "A man walking in the Amazon encountered a boy and a father in the Amazon jungle. The boy had a startling confidence in an almost frightening way. It was not a confidence like the boy had achieved something, or done something, or earned something. But a confidence that could only come from knowing in the deepest part. Knowing who he is and that he has a place in this world."[31]

The idea that this young boy knew he had a place in this world is mesmerizing.

In 2006, I was in Kabul, Afghanistan. Among the many amazing things I witnessed was seeing small seven- and eight-year-old children caring for two-year-olds. Walking incredible distances, caring for those younger children, these children had responsibilities.

Like the story of the young boy in the Amazon and the story of my dad, they knew at their core what mattered most to them and stepped in.

---

[31] Adventures Through The Mind. "Primal Parenting And The Evolved Nest W/ Darcia Narvaez, Ph.D. ~ Ep 52." YouTube video. Jul 25, 2017.

GIVING FROM STRENGTH
How do you find the courage to step in?

This is a challenging question whose answer lies in thinking of a solution together.

In the case of both the young boy in the Amazon and my dad, neither saw themselves as alone. They saw another person whose plight gave them the motivation to proceed. From a position of inner strength, they both saw another and simply stepped in.

Even when someone else is in need, that is the only thing necessary to feel a sense of place in the world and to then step in.

Conviction, determination, and deciding to live life makes all the difference. Seeing a need and stepping in fills the void.

An example of this can be found in New York City, a city of more than eight million residents. Everywhere you look, you see variety, uniqueness, and people in need.

This is the backdrop of a story that started in 2016. Two brothers, Mike and Nick Fiorito, put themselves in a place to see life in a different way and left great jobs to pursue their passion. They stepped in to make a difference while passing homeless people on the cold streets of New York. They bought and personally handed out blankets to hundreds of homeless men, women, and children across the city, tying a note of encouragement to each blanket they gave out.

"Our ultimate goal is to inspire a massive movement of kindness," Mike said.[32]

They were challenged to not just pursue corporate success but to see lives all around them and to do something, one person at a time.

Do you see the distinction?

According to the statistics of the National Alliance to End Homelessness, more than 550,000 were homeless in the United States in 2017. In the end, the homeless remained homeless. The blanket did not put food in their stomach or solve access to shelter or care. If this was a policy, it might accurately be labeled a failure.

But this is not about policy, this is about the individual. It is about you and me seeing something and being moved and stepping in. Each one, when given the blanket and the attached note, knew on that day someone noticed them. They mattered. They were cared about and important. A new life can begin from a start like this. From their inner strength, Mike and Nick gave to others, and it started a movement.

This is about connection. Mike and Nick saw people and stepped in, validating the connectedness between us all.

Seeing one person is enough to see the whole.

---

32 "Bay Ridge Brothers Partner with Schools Nationwide to Distribute 10,000." PRWeb, November 21, 2018.

RECEIVING AND SHARING STRENGTH

Mike and Nick and my dad each gave liberally to the homeless. It is the lesson of a personal connection, a personal touch in which the strength of their hearts bubbled over to the point of sharing with others.

For Mike and Nick in their non-profit effort Blankets for Hope, they added personal notes, which provided an extra individualized connection. They did not just write notes and hand them off with the blankets, they also stopped to have a conversation with each recipient. They individualized each encounter, giving dignity and worth to each one.

They saw each person as a valued part of the whole of humanity.

And my dad, at the innermost core of his person, saw a woman and children in need, homeless, begging by the side of the road, and he took action to give what he had. It was his whole world at that moment.

This is what makes me cry, seeing people being good to each other.

HOW DO YOU MEASURE SUCCESS?
1. Is it okay to find success not in things but in people? Is it okay to want to plan your life around giving to others?
2. What does it mean to not feel that way about serving people? Is it okay to want to be served? What does it mean to find joy in receiving and not giving?

CHAPTER 19

TOUCH IS THE DIFFERENCE

Touch has a memory.

—JOHN KEATS[33]

I need people. It has taken me fifty-four years to admit it. As a child, and even now as an adult, I do not like being physically touched. Or at least, I generally flinch at someone's touch when I do not know them, though I crave touch.

I am a soft-spoken introvert with an emotive personality; I sense people's feelings and project my feelings as a way of communicating. I need others to not just hear my words but to feel them, so needing people is at the center of my story of healing.

---

33 "What Can I Do to Drive Away: Poems by John Keats (1795-1821)." Accessed February 19, 2020.

Until I was a freshman in college, I did not understand why people asked me to repeat myself. I would burn with frustration whenever someone asked me to repeat myself.

"You are not listening—that is the issue. I can hear myself perfectly fine."

As a freshman, I was in a dorm with a guy I occasionally sparred with in intramural boxing. He was five inches taller and thirty pounds heavier than I was, and every time he hit me, I felt all thirty pounds of that giant lever arm! Because I knew how hard he hit, I generally tried to always stay on his good side. When he spoke, I listened. But I respected him, too; Marcus was a gentle giant.

One day while Marcus was talking to me, his voice significantly trailed off. I was focused on what he was saying, so even as his voice trailed off, I could see his lips moving and could understand the context of what he was saying. I put together in my mind what he must have said and answered him. In that moment, I understood what it must be like for others when I spoke.

LITTLE ME, BIG WORLD

When I look in the mirror, I see a complicated underachiever. Every day, I learn to live with being complicated, and I strive to thrive.

A co-worker and friend, Linda Ward, recently challenged me to consider an idea. "To grow, you must be open to receiving," she said.

The simplicity of openness has fascinated me for quite a while because I have always believed that when doors are open, opportunity and choice have the greatest potential. Doors can only be understood to be open if you are open to them being so.

I have not always been willing to see those open doors.

You have probably heard how elephants are trained to not run away. As calves, one rear leg is tied to a stake by a rope. The calf is not strong enough to pull free of the stake. Since an elephant has a long memory, it continues to associate having one rear leg tied to a stake with being unable to escape. So they stop trying.

That was me.

What was my rope, the tether that kept me from believing in what I could accomplish?

I was born prematurely. More than six weeks early, I was underweight and underdeveloped. I stayed in the neonatal intensive care unit needing help and time to grow… and then I caught pneumonia.

Little me was sick, barely clinging to life. As an infant in the 1960s, modern science kept me behind glass, cared for by doctors and nurses from a distance. On the other side of the glass, my mother was in constant prayer for me to live. I was being doubly saved.

However, I now appreciate the description given by Dr. Darcia Narvaez when she said, "When you dis-regulate a baby, you dis-regulate them for life."

My medical salvation came with a price: Without a mother's constant touch and care, I developed a sensitivity to touch.

Being skinny and little, I had never really grown, maybe because I never could. As a child, this was coupled with the fact that I was controlled by a single thought: "I am not good enough."

So I stopped trying.

As a sophomore in Abilene, Texas, I had a math teacher named Mrs. Luella E. Cochran, who told me that I was good enough, and I could do anything I wanted. Even though my mother had told me the same my whole life, it took this amazing woman I admired as an algebra teacher for me to believe it.

It changed my entire world.

Though I was already competitive, I believed I was not good enough to be what I wanted in life.

THE POWER OF TOUCH

I love getting things done.

I understand it takes a village, but I received a tough lesson in getting things done from my friend Mark when we were in high school. We were both assigned to clean the school gym after the pre-game pep-rally. I just wanted to get it done and move on. So I started giving out assignments.

"Who put you in charge?" asked Mark.

No one had put me in charge. I put me in charge, but in my mind, this question was heard as the statement, "You don't inspire others to want to follow you. You are not a natural leader."

My response in that moment would become my default life-choice: "I will do it myself."

Early on in adulthood, I would find myself on teams where I would have to inspire others. Whether that team was a family, class, faith group, or workgroup. Teams are all around us. Someone leads not only the tasks but also the group to care for one another and to want to be a group.

The truth is we all inspire one another—to give, to never give up, to believe in yourself. We inspire others to want to emulate or follow us. We inspire others to want to avoid how we handle things or to avoid us.

I have learned I am not a leader; I am a server.

Have you stopped to consider how you inspire those around you?

At the beginning of the chapter, I said, "I need people." I need people at the spiritual level because we were created in the image of God. Each human intrinsically has great worth, each one unique in history, and each person is valuable because they reflect the infinite. Our creator made us to be with Him. He wants His Holy Spirit to live in us, and we would want to be with each other, as He draws us together.

So, I say I need people because I need God at the spiritual level.

Mentally, I desire to be part of a group and to like and, in turn, be liked by others. As humans, we are social creatures and being alone is difficult. I know this to be true in my life; however, as I've shared, I am an African-American, and as a youth in Abilene, Texas, I learned that the word 'group' can be nuanced in many ways.

The idea of belonging and not belonging has been difficult.

GIVING AND RECEIVING

All my life, I have continued to have an issue with physical touch.

I'll be the first to admit it's crazy that as someone who craves physical touch and closeness, I recoil every time I am touched. The result has been standoffish-ness, which can be mistaken by some for aloofness.

But in 1995, I needed a group of men to bond like family, and I knew I had a problem that had to be overcome. As the leader of more than 150 men in Lima Company 3/1, I knew the men needed to implicitly trust each other AND me.

Trust like that doesn't come with rank or position—it comes from within. The emotional bond needed for us to go into battle, completely trusting one another above and beyond just being fellow Marines takes intentionality.

I believed the only way for them to trust me and see that I trusted them was to regularly pat them on the back.

Literally.

Most often, it was just a slap on the back or a grip of the bicep with words of encouragement. To date, I would bet none of them would recall any of those moments. They were fleeting and inconsequential. For me, however, each touch was monumental. First, because it was incredibly unnatural for me—it felt awkward and forced—because it was. Yet, I did it; I touched them individually and often.

Each touch specifically granted permission for them to touch me, though not verbally. But every single time I gave permission in my mind because I needed to consciously overcome my natural inclination to recoil when touched.

I needed them each to understand and see we were family. They could slap me on the arm or on my back or shove me on the shoulder in a joking way. I wanted my family of Marines to feel cared for and cared about. It was a giving and receiving of compassion.

I found healing in giving them permission to grow and find unity.

HOW DO YOU MEASURE RELATIONSHIPS?

1. Is it okay to feel alone in a crowded room? Is it okay to not know what to say to strangers in your own home?
2. Is it okay to feel ashamed of not knowing how to be a friend? To be among those who are different?
3. Is it okay not to find fun at a football game, an opera, or the theater? Is it okay not to enjoy chess or playing softball or golf?
4. What does it mean to feel different? What does it mean to feel the same?
5. Is it okay to be confused, feeling a little of both all the time?

CONCLUSION

The mass of men lead lives of quiet desperation.
　　　　　　　　　　　—HENRY DAVID THOREAU[34]

It is unfair not to try and then feel disappointed when nothing changes.

On my journey, I discovered that trials and difficulties should be welcomed as part of learning, and that fear should not hold me back from giving. We are all unique, and individually we should offer to the world our own abilities and insights. We are not alone, and together, we can achieve more.

In this book, I have described my journey to find an intersection between technology and purpose, to share my own struggle with purposefully approaching the rest of my life.

---

34 Thoreau, Henry David. Walden. Thomas Y. Crowell & Company, 1910.

First, we looked at Purpose:

Having a dream is what makes the sands of experience richer and able to be formed into bricks, that form walls, that form castles, that form cities and nations of opportunity!

Next, we looked at Passion:

Consider TheLastWell.org as a perfect example of what it means to inspire a generation. Find a cause worth giving your life and dedicating your talent and treasure to see it completed. Will you join in?

Next, we looked at Progress:

Faith Florez of The Latina Legacy Foundation, as a seventeen-year-old in 2017, inspired many by not letting circumstances keep her from developing a technology solution to help others who suffered under extreme temperature conditions to work smarter. This type of determination drives change for the good of all humanity.

Finally, we looked at People:

Consider Mike and Nick Fiorito and their commitment through Blankets of Hope. Theirs is also a story about you and me seeing something, being moved, and stepping in. With each blanket given to someone homeless was an attached note, so the recipient knew, on that day, someone noticed them. It is about people.

As a result of my journey, I discovered in the metaphorical desert of unknowns of the future, there exists a strong sense of purpose within each of us. As Sam Tangredi said, "When you have lost your bearings, come to all stop to discover where you are." So it is possible within the metaphorical desert, with careful navigating, to allow technology to help bring water to the desert, to find and discover what Scott Dinsmore taught, that life is meant to be lived.

During my five-year journey of discovery, I found navigation aids to help me find my way. The aids to navigation are the 4 P's—purpose, passion, progress, and people. These combine like a loadstone, giving my life compass a strong point of direction. Now that I have a guide, I can move forward confidently. I trust you can apply these in your own life, to navigate toward what you believe to be the truest direction to engage your unique talents and skills.

I'd like to end with one final important lesson—a parable about a real man who lived in the 1990s and worked as a janitor in a church. He influenced one person, and she then influenced hundreds. I heard the story at least ten years after the janitor himself had passed away after a long and fulfilling life. As I listened to the story along with thousands of other people, I am sure that, at a minimum, several thousand people were influenced. Yet I wondered what the janitor thought of his life on his deathbed. Did he think of himself as unimportant? If he did, how wrong he was! His life and influence touched thousands!

How many of us may be like the janitor in our minds, thinking we have nothing to offer and holding back. Scott

Dinsmore was right. Life is meant to be lived and enjoyed right where you are. Wherever you are, you live in the world's greatest place—go enjoy it!

Enjoy every single moment of your life, even the struggles and disappointments. Take a stand, take hold of what you believe, give deeply and passionately.

ACKNOWLEDGMENTS

I would like to thank and acknowledge the following people who have been significant friends, confidantes and mentors. They made it possible for the writing of this book to be part of the journey.

Valenda Brown (my wonderful mother)
Eric Koester (mentor and guide on the journey)
Laura Bell
Jennifer Fang Brehm
Greg Gibson
Dan Hawkins
Tish Lane Jenkins
Jim Lundsted
Jan Martin
Jon and Courtney Nadig
Monica Pampell
Jeffrey Rhoades
Michael "Buckeye" Sovacool
Ken Thewes

BIBLIOGRAPHY

CHAPTER 2

Riley, Jenelle. "Behind the Scene: How Pasek and Paul's 'Greatest Showman' Anthem 'This Is Me' Became a Smash Hit." Variety, February 21, 2018. https://variety.com/2018/film/awards/greatest-showman-this-is-me-pasek-and-paul-1202706690/.

CHAPTER 3

Frost, Robert. "The Road Not Taken." Poetry Foundation. Accessed February 18, 2020. https://www.poetryfoundation.org/poems/44272/the-road-not-taken.

CHAPTER 4

Riley, Jenelle. "Behind the Scene: How Pasek and Paul's 'Greatest Showman' Anthem 'This Is Me' Became a Smash Hit." Variety, February 21, 2018. https://variety.com/2018/film/awards/greatest-showman-this-is-me-pasek-and-paul-1202706690/.

CHAPTER 5

"Brené Brown: Create True Belonging and Heal the World." Lewis Howes, February 11, 2020. https://lewishowes.com/podcast/r-brene-brown-create-true-belonging-and-heal-the-world/.

EisseCatherine Wade. "The Power Of Vulnerability | Brené Brown | TED Talks". YouTube video. Aug 7, 2016. https://www.youtube.com/watch?v=pXb8AQOONgE&feature=youtu.be.

Trafton, Anne. "In the Blink of an Eye." MIT News, January 16, 2014. http://news.mit.edu/2014/in-the-blink-of-an-eye-0116.

CHAPTER 6

Harris, José N. *Mi Vida: a Story of Faith, Hope and Love*. (United States: Xlibris Corporation, 2010).

CHAPTER 7

Ewing, Audrey. "Think Millennials Have 'Issues," Just Wait for Gen Z." Audrey, January 10, 2019. http://audreyewing.com/think-millennials-have-issues-just-wait-for-gen-z/.

CHAPTER 8

NDTV. "Full Transcript: In Conversation with Oprah Winfrey." NDTV.com, January 23, 2012. https://www.ndtv.com/india-news/full-transcript-in-conversation-with-oprah-winfrey-568399.

"Passion." Merriam-Webster. Merriam-Webster. Accessed February 18, 2020. https://www.merriam-webster.com/dictionary/passion.

CHAPTER 9

Kaiser, Shannon. "3 Unexpected Ways to Find Your Life Purpose." HuffPost. HuffPost, September 25, 2017. https://www.huffpost.com/entry/3-unexpected-ways-to-find_b_5176511.

Walton, Paul A. O'Keefe, Carol Dweck, and Greg Walton. "Having a Growth Mindset Makes It Easier to Develop New Interests." Harvard Business Review, September 11, 2018. https://hbr.org/2018/09/having-a-growth-mindset-makes-it-easier-to-develop-new-interests.

CHAPTER 11

The Joint Congressional Committee on Inaugural Ceremonies." Franklin D. Roosevelt Inaugural Address. March 4, 1933. Accessed February 18, 2020. https://www.inaugural.senate.gov/about/past-inaugural-ceremonies/37th-inaugural-ceremonies/.

CHAPTER 12

Battaglia, Roberto, Nick Skillicorn, Leo Bottary, Nick Skillicorn, Mike Steffes, Derek White, Xaver Wiesmann, and Hayley Bagnall. "What Is Innovation? 15 Experts Share Their Innovation Definition." Idea to Value, November 4, 2016. https://www.ideatovalue.com/inno/nickskillicorn/2016/03/innovation-15-experts-share-innovation-definition/.

CHAPTER 13

O'Keefe, Paul A., Carol S. Dweck, and Gregory M. Walton. "Implicit Theories of Interest: Finding Your Passion or Developing It?" Psychological Science 29, no. 10 (October 2018): 1653–64. doi:10.1177/0956797618780643.

Wilde, Oscar. *The Decay of Lying: a Dialogue.* London: K. Paul, Trench, 1889.

CHAPTER 14

Goodell, Jeff. "Steve Jobs in 1994: The Rolling Stone Interview." *Rolling Stone*, June 25, 2018. https://www.rollingstone.com/culture/culture-news/steve-jobs-in-1994-the-rolling-stone-interview-231132/.

Simón, Yara. "This Teen Invented Calor, An App That Aims to Keep Farmworkers Safe in Hot Weather." Remezcla, April 11, 2018. https://remezcla.com/culture/faith-florez-app-farmworkers-safe/.

CHAPTER 15

Tweney, Dylan. "Dec. 9, 1968: The Mother of All Demos." Wired. Conde Nast, September 11, 2018. https://www.wired.com/2010/12/1209computer-mouse-mother-of-all-demos/.

CHAPTER 16

Kickstarter. "Tina Roth Eisenberg: The Best Way To Complain Is To Make Things." YouTube video. Nov 16, 2016. https://www.youtube.com/watch?v=rUtABHdlAzg&feature=youtu.be.

CHAPTER 17

Orwell, George. *Burmese Days*. Place of publication not identified: Houghton Mifflin Harcourt, 1974.

Stiffler, Lisa. "Interview: Candace Faber, Seattle's First 'Civic Technology Advocate,' on Tech for Change, and How to Save Seattle." GeekWire, August 11, 2016. https://www.geekwire.com/2016/interview-candace-faber-seattles-first-civic-technology-advocate-tech-change-save-seattle/.

CHAPTER 18

Adventures Through The Mind. "Primal Parenting And The Evolved Nest W/ Darcia Narvaez, Ph.D. ~ Ep 52." YouTube video. Jul 25, 2017. https://www.youtube.com/watch?v=aCyWMRhMlV0.

"Bay Ridge Brothers Partner with Schools Nationwide to Distribute 10,00." PRWeb, November 21, 2018. https://www.prweb.com/releases/bay_ridge_brothers_partner_with_schools_nationwide_to_distribute_10_000_blankets_to_the_homeless/prweb15939378.htm.

Catholic Online. "Mother Teresa Quotes - Mother Teresa of Calcutta." Catholic Online. Accessed February 19, 2020. https://www.catholic.org/clife/teresa/quotes.php.

CHAPTER 19

"What Can I Do to Drive Away: Poems by John Keats (1795-1821)." Go back to the front page. Poems by John Keats (1795-1821).

Accessed February 19, 2020. http://keats-poems.com/tag/what-can-i-do-to-drive-away/.

CONCLUSION
Thoreau, Henry David. *Walden*. Thomas Y. Crowell & Company, 1910.

www.ingramcontent.com/pod-product-compliance
Lightning Source LLC
LaVergne TN
LVHW011825060526
838200LV00053B/3903